Losing and Finding My Father

Losing and Finding
My Father

SEASONS OF GRIEF,
HEALING AND FORGIVENESS

Kira Freed

Foreword by Richard C. Schwartz, PhD

Two Hawks Press
Tucson, AZ

Losing and Finding My Father:
Seasons of Grief, Healing and Forgiveness

Copyright © 2015 by Kira Freed

All rights reserved.

This book recommends activities for wellness but is by no means
a substitute for medical or psychiatric care.

Song lyrics on page 116 used with permission from Bill Staines. Quotation
on page 237 used with permission from Deborah Daw Heffernan. Exercise
on pages 247–248 adapted with permission from Piero Ferrucci. "The Four
Approaches to Forgiveness" on pages 263–264 used with permission from
Janis Abrahms Spring. All reasonable efforts have been made to contact
the copyright holder of the song lyrics on page vii and the author of the
quotations on pages 235 and 238.

Author photo by Charlie Alolkoy

Two Hawks Press
www.twohawkspress.com

ISBN: 978-0-6923170-9-9

Printed in the United States of America

For my father,
Lou Silverberg,
1916–1991

and

for Paul Bowman
with deepest thanks

So I'll tell you that I love you even though I'm far away
And I'll tell you how you change me as I live from day to day
How you help me to accept myself and I won't forget to say
Love is never wasted, even when it's hard love

Yes, it's hard love, but it's love all the same
Not the stuff of fantasy, but more than just a game
And the only kind of miracle that's worthy of the name
For the love that heals our lives is mostly hard love

Table of Contents

Foreword

Humans are unique among animals in the length of our dependence on our parents. As attachment theorists have demonstrated, this lengthy vulnerability gives one or both parents the ability to powerfully shape our internal world for our lifetime. A violently abusive parent will create inner polarizations between aspects of us that were terrified and enraged versus aspects that desperately longed for the parent's love, clung to the tender moments, excused or minimized the abuse, or blamed ourselves.

If they don't work to heal, most survivors of such abuse become dominated by one or the other set of extreme emotions and live accordingly. That is, they either become loners, swearing never again to be so vulnerable, or they plunge into a series of abusive relationships that resemble the one with the abusive parent as they search for a parent surrogate who will love them the way the parent didn't.

The death of an abusive parent will expose these conflicts in a hurricane of confusing emotions. Because the parent is no longer a threat, the loner's terror may suddenly abate, the rage may relax, and the needy emotions that had been exiled rush forward. With that shift comes intense grief and hopelessness—while the parent was living, there was always the chance to get from him or her what was needed. Now that can never happen.

Most people are not this clear about what they are experiencing. All they know is that suddenly they are in intense pain. Most run from this turmoil, finding ways to numb or distract themselves until the storm blows over.

Those people are missing a huge opportunity for healing. Their inner fortress has cracked open, and they have a chance to become acquainted with and unburden the highly vulnerable emotions that were contained within it. They can also listen to the fear and anger without being triggered by the parent's existence and can help those extreme emotions relax for good.

When her father was dying, Kira Freed had the courage to take the healing path. Her carefully and beautifully documented journey provides a model for anyone who might consider this difficult route. She embraces the emotions that we all want to escape and, in doing so, releases the extreme beliefs that had constrained her life for so long. By immersing ourselves in her experience, we see that such healing is possible and are inspired to relate in a similar way to aspects of ourselves that we fear. As we develop a new relationship with those aspects, we come to a sense of peace beyond what we ever suspected was possible.

Richard C. Schwartz, PhD
Developer of the Internal Family Systems model of psychotherapy and author or coauthor of seven books, including the most widely read family therapy text, and over sixty professional articles

Introduction

My father and I were not good friends. He was a fierce, passionate man who fought injustice in the world while wreaking havoc inside our home. I was terrified of him for over a decade. I was outraged for another three. And then he was gone, before I had a chance to make peace.

My father died on March 7, 1991, at the age of seventy-four. After a weeklong hospital stay in early January for an episode of cardiac fibrillation, he experienced another episode the following week. On doctor's orders, my parents called an ambulance for transport to Cleveland's Mt. Sinai Medical Center. The ambulance medic, who had difficulty starting and securing an IV, asked for help from the ungloved driver-medic. This unsterile situation is presumed to have caused a staph infection at the IV site that traveled throughout my father's bloodstream, severely affecting his memory and brain function. For two weeks, a team of specialists struggled to control the infection, which eventually settled and mushroomed on a weakened heart valve. On January 24, he underwent surgery for a valve replacement.

He appeared to come through surgery successfully, and his condition looked encouraging. His doctors predicted that he would be comatose for at least a few days because of the seriousness of the procedure. Over the next week, his vital signs were strong, and his heart was healing well. The only problem was that he wasn't waking up.

My father remained comatose during the month of February. Day after day, I sat at his bedside, hoping my familiar voice would call him back to waking. I imagined him well and hoped that the power of my prayers could make it so, even though the gasping ventilator and bandaged incision running the length of his chest were constant reminders of the grievous assault on his body and spirit. Various doctors shared encouraging news and dire prognoses. Hope and despair swirled through me many times each day. I tried my best just to stay present.

During those weeks, I was physically closer to my father than I'd been in decades for more than a guarded hug or to work alongside him stacking logs onto a winter woodpile. I massaged the soles of his feet and touched his ankles, hairless and soft as the skin of a newborn. I stroked his arms, rounded my hand over the warm top of his head, placed my hand on his heart and felt the steady beat. I marveled that no flash of lightning struck me as if to proclaim that one can never, ever get this close to one's father.

After five weeks with no change in his condition, my father's neurologist eventually ordered more tests that disclosed considerable brain damage caused by infected matter migrating from his heart to his brain before and during surgery. His medical team determined that the brain damage was so extensive that my father would never recover a meaningful quality of life. Certain that he wouldn't want to live under such circumstances, my family made the decision to execute his living will and discontinue life support. He died six weeks after surgery.

I was thirty-nine when my father died. It never crossed my mind that I would lose either of my parents so young. In addition, some part of me didn't believe anything—not even death—could defeat my invincible father. Although he hadn't been actively involved in my life for nearly twenty years and our relationship was difficult at best, he was a towering presence in my psyche, one whose influence had shaped and still colored my self-concept and life choices in powerful ways.

Losing my father triggered a tangle of grief that took three years to unravel. Despite recommendations from friends and acquaintances to "get on with my life," I was utterly absorbed in my grieving. At first this absorption was outside my control and I was helpless to resist it. As I came to understand my grieving as a life-altering passage, I actively embraced the process. Having come through to the other side, I feel blessed to have made this transformative pilgrimage.

My writing began as solace for the pain of losing my father, a cathartic way to release the nightmares and honor the sacred times. I didn't understand rationally why I needed to write—I only knew that when I gave voice to the stories, I could live more peacefully, having captured a poignant experience or named a piece of my distress. Most of all, I wrote because I couldn't stop writing. In the months after my father's death, I would awaken at 4:00 a.m., my mind swimming with hospital images of him crying or in pain, interspersed with tender exchanges between us. Or I'd wake up panting from a dream in which I'd been frantic to determine the cause of his coma so he could receive treatment and recover. The only way to keep from being flooded all day by those emotions and images was to write them down. This story tugged at me to be told, and I could only allow it to emerge.

Over time I realized that others might want to learn about my healing journey. The night a friend finished reading an early draft, he had a dream in which he was celebrating Mass for his father, who had died twenty years earlier. Another friend shared that my writing helped him come to terms with his abusive upbringing. A cousin said that my story helped her understand how to be fully present when her daughter was dying. I hoped that my story might be useful to others as well.

Books about bereavement often discuss the stages of grieving and the emotions to be expected. One of my intentions in writing this book has been to present an organic rather than textbook account of feelings and issues that surfaced, as well as threads of personal history that wove into the grieving. (Because this book is a memoir and not simply an account of my father's death, my story begins with his childhood in order to trace cultural and generational influences on our relationship and my grief and healing.) My friend Phil once described his sense that when his father died, everything in his life flew up in the air, and it was up to him to figure out how to put the pieces back together. I had no inkling that so many pieces of my life would be unearthed—early childhood memories of being alone, my relationship with my body, my choice not to have children, and more. I include them all in order to tell the fullest possible story instead of leaving out pieces not specific to what people commonly think of as the grieving process. *All* of this is the grieving process, and allowing it to cover the broadest range of feelings and experiences brings more of me to the task of healing. I share my experiences in hopes that readers will take whatever is relevant to their lives and release the rest. My only assertion about universality is that profound levels of insight are available during times of significant loss.

∽

This book is about learning to swim in the deep waters of emotion. It recounts a three-year experience of opening to grief and following an inner call to healing. Since I'd never before lost someone close, I had no idea what grieving was about, yet I felt a constant tug of emotions that sought expression and release. As I grew to trust that following their wisdom would lead to resolution, I surrendered to the turbulent currents of my emotions. Profound healing followed.

The process of grieving my father's death and learning to welcome my emotions didn't come naturally. I had erected strong defenses growing up with a father from whom I needed to protect myself, both physically and emotionally. The physical abuse, which began when I was seven, felt like a volcano erupting with no warning—no shaking of the earth, not even a faint plume of smoke to hint at what was to come. My child's mind could see no connection between my actions and the chaos that followed; I only knew that my father sometimes turned violent and that I was helpless to avoid his rage.

In my most vivid memory of his violence, he took me into his bedroom, pulled down my pants, and whipped me with his belt. I have no recollection of what I might have done to provoke his rage, and no sense of what any child could do to deserve that kind of treatment. I have only a clear memory of being helpless in the presence of his tall, muscled frame—a terror-stricken rag doll. I also remember the blistered red welts on my backside. My sister Rowan, five years younger, joked for years that they looked like hot dogs. I suspect her humor helped deflect the gravity of the warning those welts represented to her: *Stay in line, or you're next.*

Around the same time, my brother and I were in the kitchen one evening, bickering as we washed the dinner dishes. Our father burst into the room, shoved Mark roughly into a corner, and struck him hard several times. I crouched in the opposite corner, frozen in fear, praying to become invisible so I could evade my father's tornadic fury, yet compelled to stay and witness the violence in order to burn into my memory the consequences of crossing him. That terror still lives in my body.

My father came from a poor Jewish family and worked in the meat business. He was six feet three and walked stiffly due to a chronically aching back. He had a commanding presence and a ready sense of humor, replete with foreign accents—the good looks of Gregory Peck combined with the playful wit of Danny Kaye. His trimmed beard and mustache complemented a furry halo of dark hair. In honey-colored corduroys, a Pendleton shirt, and sheepskin-lined moccasins, he looked like an animated college professor or a well-groomed seaman.

But I knew another side of him. He had fiery eyes, a raging temper, and a thousand things that set him off. A jacket lying on a chair for two minutes, a plate left unwashed after lunch. Giggling on road trips. Phone calls during the dinner hour. Children awake after 9:00 p.m. Introspection or controversy at the dinner table. Discussion, disagreement, disobedience. Any hint of chaos, any challenge to his authority.

Enduring years of my father's rage conditioned me to a life of hypervigilance, reading his every facial expression, gesture, and tone of voice in hopes of defusing his moods before they escalated into violence. Although I rarely perceived any connection between my actions and his explosions, I quickly learned that silence and supreme obedience were smart strategies. By the time I reached my teens, fear had become so sufficient a control mechanism that he needed only to shoot me a steely glare and I was as well behaved as a beaten dog.

In my inner world, however, things were different. I understood clearly that my father's behavior was not warranted. I escaped the trap that devours the self-esteem of many abused children: believing it's their fault, that they're bad, that they must deserve the violence or it wouldn't be happening. Internalizing the "badness" allows children to believe that the people charged with their safety and well-being know what they're doing; to believe otherwise is to abandon all semblance of sanity in one's life, an intolerable option for children and one that most will unconsciously sacrifice their self-esteem to avoid.

I was extremely fortunate to be able to preserve a clear sense of my own goodness in the face of my father's abuse. From early on, I had a strong core and an awareness that my tender nature was a gift, regardless of how others treated me. Still, the onslaught of rage and violence eventually took a toll. After my father's death I came to understand that, in childhood, I developed what I call my "shield of hatred." No one understood or honored me, no one looked out for my best interests—therefore no one was to be trusted. While I was growing up, this was true. To generalize it to an adult worldview, although a natural consequence of my conditioning, was lethal to my sense of humanity.

This shield of hatred, developed as an unconscious strategy to protect me from my father, created strong internal walls that kept out immediate dangers, yet left me unable to feel authentic emotions. I became so proficient at blocking the hurt that I grew to adulthood incapable of being vulnerable or experiencing intimacy in my life. My relationships were built on the shaky ground of anger, mistrust, and control. I had become an expert at slamming doors and walking away, each time invigorated by the resulting sense of freedom. I now understand my behavior as a need to compulsively practice what I wasn't allowed to do as a child— say no.

In my late thirties, my defenses began to crack. Living in San Francisco, I awoke early on the morning of October 17, 1989, with the words *Be prepared to die today* floating in my thoughts. I couldn't imagine their meaning and tried to forget them as I went about my day. With late afternoon came a magnitude 7.1 earthquake. Although badly shaken, I suffered no physical injury. During the days that followed, I reflected on the words that had come to me. *Be prepared to die today.* I became aware that my world needed to be metaphorically cracked open, that the core of my personality needed shaking up in order to awaken me to change and growth. Although I didn't consciously know what in me required shaking up, I affirmed my willingness to open to the process—to let this earthquake break apart whatever I carried inside that kept me from living fully, and to allow the old "me" to die so that a new "me" could be born.

At the time, I had just entered a master's program in counseling psychology at California Institute of Integral Studies, an innovative graduate school in San Francisco that integrates academic, experiential, and spiritual wisdom in its educational approach. As part of the program, I was encouraged to participate in individual therapy. The curriculum was emotionally rigorous and guaranteed to bring personal issues to the surface, and as a responsible psychotherapist, I would need to be aware enough of my own unresolved issues to distinguish them from those of my clients. Soon after entering the program, I was referred by a professor-friend to Paul Bowman, a PhD graduate of the same school who was a gifted therapist. I'd worked with therapists several times since my late teens, but I'd never before sensed the match to be good enough to go to the core of the healing work I needed to do. With Paul, that became possible. We began our work together the week of the earthquake and over time laid a firm foundation for processing the barrage of emotions that surfaced around my father's death seventeen months later.

Paul was a tall, lanky, slightly balding man several years younger than I whose mild demeanor concealed an intensity I grew to treasure. Passionately aligned with a client's internal healing force, he practiced an insightful balance of deep empathy and unflinching determination to get to the heart of emotional wounds—to bring them to consciousness so they could begin to heal. His therapeutic style blended an empowering psychodynamic approach (self psychology, developed by Heinz Kohut) with encouragement to develop an "observer self" able to step back, witness, and name the truth of an experience. Added to the mix was complete permission to express emotions in an environment free of shame—quite the opposite of my childhood, when I was regularly told to quit being a crybaby or go to my room until I calmed down. Paul's deep trust in the healing process and his understanding of its components helped me embrace my authenticity as the road to my healing. My work with Paul also counteracted my childhood strategy of keeping myself apart from others since no one was a safe haven. Over time, Paul's ability to create a compassionate container for our work cracked the code of my isolation.

I looked forward to my weekly sessions in Paul's office in an old Victorian house in San Francisco's Sunset District. I'd sit in the waiting room, sipping peppermint tea and reviewing my focus for the session. Sometimes the topic appeared full-blown, while at other times it was only a tidbit of a dream or memory begging for attention. And sometimes I didn't have a clue until Paul opened the door, welcoming me into his spacious, sunny office. Then the safety of his caring presence drew out whatever had risen to the top over the past week, whatever emotions and concerns were ready to receive healing attention.

Therapy taught me to acknowledge my walled-off feelings. I came to understand that I wasn't there to "look good" for Paul or to impress him with my strengths. As I grew to trust him, I learned, little by little, to share aspects of my life that *weren't* working—my loneliness from lack of an intimate partner, my inability to draw love into my life, my perennial longing for more closeness with my family, insecurities about my identity as a woman, issues about weight and body image, and more. Over time, as I allowed Paul into my inner world and revealed my vulnerable side, I discovered the power of speaking the truth of my life: my feelings, my experiences, my yearnings. Speaking the truth meant bringing those things into awareness, and when I did, the natural healing energies of life took over and transformed the pain into insights and tools for living. For several years this process required Paul's supportive assistance as facilitator. As I continue to grow in understanding and self-acceptance, I become increasingly able to be my own facilitator while remaining open to outside help as needed.

These healing energies had much more in mind for me than I could have imagined. Before my father's illness and death, my relationship with him was riddled with discord and a longing for closeness and trust that had always eluded me. Through periods of conflict, silence, avoidance, and rough, tentative efforts to connect, we barely maintained a state of peace. He considered me crazy for changing my college major from psychology to anthropology, and even crazier for moving to Ithaca, New York, in 1982 without having a job lined up in advance. He didn't like my clothes, my boyfriends, my vagabond ways. I'd been on my own for nearly twenty years, yet he still treated me like a teenager.

I had no idea that the process of grieving would heal not only the loss of my father to death but also the losses inherent in a relationship filled with deep hurts and long-standing wounds. The healing energies also came to touch other aspects of my life that were byproducts of my relationship with my father, in particular the ways my adaptations to that relationship kept me in a pattern of distrusting men and avoiding intimacy. As I immersed myself in my pain with no timetable, not only did the grief subside, but along with it went my sense of having had a bad father. My anger and resentment were replaced by deep, openhearted love for him.

My hard feelings toward him began to melt as I sat at his hospital bedside. I'd grown up aching for a father who was gentle, and in our last days together that wish was granted. He was stripped to his elemental self by a critical illness that brought his vulnerability to the surface. I softened in the safety that his softness created. My anger at him became tempered with compassion as I learned to respect the forces that had shaped his life, causing him to be violent and withhold love. My anger at myself for having become so defended was replaced by that same compassion as I acknowledged the challenging conditions in which I grew up. Over time, my capacity for intimacy expanded, which allowed me to finally venture into the territory of committed relationship. If I had been told that all this rich healing would emerge from my father's death, I would not have believed it. But after diving into the dark waters of grief and coming to this sense of inner peace, I now believe it—and give great thanks for both the journey and the fruits it has borne.

Some of what I've written about my father is angry and some is loving. My grieving brought to the surface a full range of emotions, and I include them all here. I didn't write this book with the intention of portraying my father as "the bad guy" and myself as "the wronged child." Every parent has made mistakes, as has every child, and with perfect hindsight we'd all conduct ourselves differently. Each of us inherits challenges and life lessons through the alchemical mixture of personalities, strengths, and wounds between parent and child. There are a thousand ways to deny support to a child, and a thousand reasons why it happens. Likewise, there are a thousand ways to mend from assaults on a tender spirit. The essential lesson is simply to begin the healing journey. My goal has never been to assign right or wrong—simply to recount my experiences and share some of the ways I've found to work through my childhood issues and move beyond them.

Some people may wonder why I'd go public with my painful relationship with my father. When we as humans don't learn from our struggles, the pain and suffering are a big waste—just more evidence that "life sucks and then we die." When we grow as a result of the strife, we honor its purpose as well as its gifts. The healing between my father and me was a remarkable and profoundly

CHAPTER I

My Father's History

My father was the child of Jewish immigrants from Poland, which was then under the oppressive rule of the Russian Czarist Empire. Most Polish Jews lived in ghettos and were targets of prejudice, hatred, and violence.

The marriage of my father's parents, Bessie Brooker (known to us as Bubu) and Joseph Zylberberg (later changed to Silverberg), was arranged by Bubu's father, as was the custom. He chose Joseph for a son-in-law because no dowry was expected. Bubu had been in love with another man but couldn't disobey her father's wishes, so she entered into a loveless marriage. Bubu's father subscribed to the old-school convention of cherishing sons and devaluing daughters, so Bubu's brothers received educational and other opportunities that were denied to her and her sisters. As the oldest daughter, Bubu was treated like a servant, bearing the brunt of household chores and care of her younger siblings. Although extremely intelligent—she possessed an innate sense of psychology and was consulted regularly by family members for advice—she never learned to read or write.

Joseph enjoyed a comfortable childhood, raised by loving parents who owned a successful lumber business. He was well educated and fluent in Russian, Polish, Hungarian, Yiddish, and Hebrew. (He later took night-school classes to learn English but wrote the language phonetically.) Joseph fell in love with Bubu—a relationship fully supported by his parents—and apprenticed to her father, eventually becoming a blacksmith. Joseph and Bubu married and had two sons, Ed and Ben, while still in Poland. In 1904, Joseph immigrated to the United States, leaving Poland to escape the pogroms and avoid conscription into the Russian army. His destination was Cleveland because his traveling companion knew people there. After arriving, he learned that his parents, who had remained in Poland, had been robbed and murdered. The money from their lumber business, hidden in the house, was an easy target for thieves. Everyone in the house was killed except for a young boy who rolled in a comforter and hid under a bed. He was able to identify the murderers, who were hanged for their crime.

Joseph initially worked in an ironworks factory, but he soon opened his own blacksmith shop, where crowds would gather to watch him shoe horses and repair wagons. Within a year after immigrating, Joseph's financial success allowed him to send for Bubu and their two young sons as well as her parents, who all arrived in 1905. By 1916, Bubu had borne four more children—Morris, Sonny (who died at age five), Rose, and Lou, my father, who was the youngest.

The family settled in the Woodland area of Cleveland's east side, a neighborhood of Eastern European immigrants steeped in Old World culture where the traditional patriarchal system set the tone. Men ruled the family and struggled to bring in money, while women raised the children, cooked, baked, cleaned, and volunteered with charity organizations. Painfully aware that it was a man's world, Bubu celebrated the birth of each of her sons and regretted the birth of her only daughter for what Rose would have to endure.

During the early decades of the 1900s, women rarely worked outside the home, but many, including Bubu, took in boarders to earn extra income. When Rose was very young, extended family members newly arrived from Europe stayed in the house until they got settled and found work. When Rose was a teenager in the late 1920s, Bubu often opened their home to friends experiencing domestic discord or "down on their luck." Rose once described the house as being like Grand Central Station: "You never knew who'd be sharing your bedroom or who needed a meal on any given night."

The values of the European ghetto—respect for education, music, and family life—were brought to America and, despite the poverty, were fostered in children by schools and settlement houses. Child-rearing practices also reflected the Eastern European Jewish culture. Children were not the center of attention; they were expected to behave, follow orders, be helpful, and stay out of trouble. Superstitious belief in the evil eye prohibited calling attention to the good in one's life for fear that it would be cursed or taken away. Children weren't directly acknowledged for their positive qualities, such as intelligence or beauty, nor for their achievements, such as good grades in school. Praise was given in a backhanded manner—"not so bad" or "so-so" with a teasing air—rather than a straightforward "That was wonderful!" or "How talented you are!" Declarations of love were absent; emotional expression wasn't the custom, neither toward children nor between husband and wife.

Corporal punishment was the accepted method of discipline. Children were accustomed to being hit or strapped by their parents, and teachers had the authority to paddle a disobedient child or rap knuckles with a ruler. However, Joseph's cruel and violent behavior exceeded the bounds of normal discipline, both within the family and outside of it. Stories have been told of him slashing the tires on his neighbor's car and hitting a man hard enough to knock out his teeth. My father had vivid memories of his father's enormous blacksmith hands and the frequent beatings he received for misbehaving and for not practicing the violin. Rose, exempt from her father's violence as the only daughter, described Joseph's disciplinary method with the boys as the Law of the Razor Strap. Whether he used it or simply showed it as a threat, he got results.

My father grew up afraid of his father, more so when Joseph's violence toward him escalated as he entered his teen years. Rose recalled that my father would hide behind her when Joseph came after him because he knew that Joseph would never touch Rose. In addition to feeling bitter about the terror he suffered, my father resented Joseph's poor treatment of Bubu. Joseph blocked opportunities for Bubu to get an education, believing he'd lose control of her. He also accused her of stealing money from Ben, the second son, a gifted violinist who was earning a respectable living.

The older sons feared their father's violence when they discovered that he owned a gun. In 1929, when Bubu's sister's exhusband was invited for a Sabbath meal, Joseph beat him with brass knuckles because he believed the man was giving Bubu too much attention. Ed, the oldest son, said, "That's it—he can't live here anymore."

Bubu and Joseph divorced and stopped talking to each other, but Bubu couldn't bring herself to evict him, so he simply moved to the third floor of the house. He ate at a nearby restaurant but was included when company came to visit, and few people were aware that the two had divorced. Bubu and Joseph communicated through their children. "Tell your father the kitchen sink needs fixing." "You need a new coat? Tell your father." Joseph used his children to put Bubu down for being illiterate. "Your report card needs signing? Tell your mother to sign it."

My father was an average student who studied the violin and spent time with his friends. He was an avid reader, but school held no interest for him. At age sixteen, in the midst of the Depression, he dropped out and began working. (In his fifties, he returned to school, proudly earning a high school diploma. He joked that perhaps he'd go on to graduate school and become a psychiatrist.)

My father married his first wife, Ruth, when he was twenty-two, and they had two girls, Diane (Deedee) and Kathie. I once asked why he married her. He stated simply, "It was the thing to do at the time," indicating that he was following a prescription for adulthood—get married and have children—rather than his heart's desire. He always spoke of Ruth with respect but implied more than once that she, too, was simply doing what was expected.

Ruth's heart had been weakened by childhood rheumatic fever, and she died suddenly at age twenty-nine when the girls were four and two. Several months later, Lou reconnected with my mother, Bea, whom he'd dated thirteen years earlier. The sparks of friendship and romance rekindled easily, and they married in 1949, six months after Ruth's death.

CHAPTER 2

My Mother's History

M
y mother's parents immigrated to the United States as teen-
agers—her mother, Deborah (Dora) Hahn, from Hungary
and her father, Louis Friedman, from eastern Slovakia. Both Hungary and Slovakia belonged to the Austro-Hungarian Empire,
where the political and cultural climate for Jews was less oppressive than in Poland, where my father's parents were from.

The two families settled in the Pittsburgh area, where Dora and
Louis later met. Their sweet courtship was evidenced by his love
letters to her, which my mother read many years later. The letters
began with "My dear Miss Hahn" and ended with "My dearest
darling." As the romance blossomed, he wrote of his desire to hold
her close and his yearning for them to share their lives.

After marrying, Dora moved from Pittsburgh to Akron, Ohio,
where Louis now lived. They settled in a modest middle-class
neighborhood where Jews made up only five percent of the population. Dora and Louis were important members of their community, which was centered around the small Hungarian Orthodox
Jewish synagogue they helped to establish. Dora was a woman
of strength and integrity who modeled respect and compassion.
My mother once described her as ". . . a modest yet self-affirming
woman, grounded in her deep spiritual beliefs and a commitment
to serving family and community. Her luminous black eyes conveyed her compassion for young and old, and she was held in
deep respect for her wisdom and honesty."

Dora was a devoted mother to her two daughters, Eleanor, born in 1916, and Bea, my mother, born in 1919. Louis was a sweet, gentle man and a good father who worked hard to earn a living, which was particularly difficult during the Depression era. He co-owned Ohio Paper and Notion Company, a small but successful wholesale store.

The love that Dora and Louis felt for each other was evident in their manner and actions, and they were seen as a warm, close couple. They displayed their feelings for their daughters with hugs and kisses as well as with the clear message "I love you." Although Louis was often teasing in his expressions of affection, my mother recalled growing up feeling the strong support and caring of both parents. In addition, Dora's large extended family reinforced that the girls were special, adored, and cherished. Discipline came in the form of an occasional smack as a reminder to behave, but nothing severe enough to instill fear.

Eleanor was the "good child" who did what was expected, while my mother—a rambunctious, sports-oriented tomboy—became the "son" her father had always wanted. In her words, she ". . . grew up following [her] father around like a puppy dog, intent on discovering the mysteries of washing a car, fixing an electrical wall plug, and tossing a baseball like a real boy." She dreamed of having a toolbox of her own and insisted on wearing her cousin Irwin's pants or asking her mother to buy boys' pants for her. (During the late 1920s, girls' pants weren't available in stores.) Cousin Irwin, her surrogate brother, was a frail, scared kid; she beat up the neighborhood boys who mocked him.

During her college years in the late 1930s, my mother excelled in sports—basketball, volleyball, and badminton—and earned an athletic letter. She gradually transferred her mastery in sports to intellectual mastery, declaring, "I was going to be as smart as any man." She honed her intellect and prided herself on it.

During this time, she began to espouse politically progressive beliefs that have guided her thinking throughout her life. Her political orientation and love of learning led her to follow a path that was unusual for a small-town Jewish girl who was expected to get married and have babies. Graduate studies in history on a scholarship to the University of Chicago gave her wings to seek work that fostered her commitment to a peaceful, just world, first in Washington, D.C., during World War II, and immediately after in Yugoslavia with the United Nations Relief and Rehabilitation Administration (UNRRA). Photos from that time portray a vibrant, self-assured woman of medium height with animated eyes, a strong nose and warm smile, wavy black hair, and a curvaceous body that she inhabited comfortably. She was idealistic, fiercely committed to causes, and fascinated by people, both individually and culturally.

My mother returned to the United States in July of 1947 after UNRRA closed down. Two months later she settled in New York City, moving into a refurbished Greenwich Village brownstone owned by a friend with whom she had worked in Washington, D.C., during the war. Many of the apartments were inhabited by colleagues who had served overseas on postwar assignments, and she continued to be part of a community of people dedicated to international peace. She worked with National Artists, Scientists, and Professionals, a politically progressive group of peace-minded activists led by Lillian Hellman, W. E. B. DuBois, and others who were trying to mobilize people against the direction of the Cold War and the infringement of civil liberties.

CHAPTER 3

Marriage and Early Family Life

My parents first met in 1936 at the Akron wedding of my mother's sister, Ellie, to Jack Magilavy, whose family was close with my father's family. My mother was a freshman at Akron University, and my father worked for meager wages at Joseph and Feis, a clothing manufacturer. He couldn't afford a car, so he traveled by bus from Cleveland to Akron on weekends, staying with Jack and Ellie, to date my mother. They picnicked, hiked, canoed, and played baseball, but neither one was in love. My father was recovering from a serious love affair, and my mother was absorbed in her college studies, so they drifted apart.

In the spring of 1949, my father was living in Ashtabula, a small town in rural northeastern Ohio. He had lost his first wife, Ruth, several months earlier. My mother, who lived in Greenwich Village, traveled to Akron for Passover and stayed with her parents, who shared a duplex with Ellie and Jack. The first afternoon of her visit, Ellie and Jack came upstairs with my father, who was visiting. When he asked my mother to go to dinner, she replied that she never turned down a free meal. They went out, saw each other the following day, and corresponded after she returned to New York.

Within a few weeks he flew to New York for a visit and soon after made several more trips, during which time things "steamed up" (my mother's words). By early June, she visited for a weekend in Ashtabula, where Bubu was caring for the household. My father proposed marriage, but my mother was undecided because she couldn't understand what she was feeling and didn't trust anything that she couldn't figure out rationally. In her words,

> *Lou came to New York the following weekend, and when he left he said that if I wanted to marry him, I would have to call him. He later told, with bravado, how he lay in the bathtub on Tuesday evening, and when Bubu said I was on the phone, he said, "She's going to marry me!"*
>
> *He came to New York, and we called my mom and dad. Mom asked when we were getting married, and I turned to Lou and he said, "Next week." Well, no way, because Mom had to bake strudel, so we set it for July 10. I went home that next week and bought a pearl gray chiffon dress (my mom thought I would get married in jeans) and a tangerine silk shantung dress. We married at my mom and dad's house on that Sunday with all the family and with Rabbi Hartstein officiating.*

My mother left Greenwich Village to settle into married life with my father in Ashtabula. He had moved there from Cleveland in 1942 with Ruth to join Ruth's father in the steel scrap business. After the war, when Ruth's brother returned from military service, he and my father formed the Ashtabula Glass Company, which specialized in auto and construction glass.

My father, recently widowed, was busy earning a living and caring for his two young daughters. After ten years of marriage, he had become accustomed to the traditional domestic scene. For my mother, however, married life and parenthood were enormous changes from her life as a political activist and free spirit. The challenges grew even greater when more children came along—Mark in 1950, I in 1951, and Rowan in 1956.

The adjustments challenged them both. My father was accustomed to a wife who said, "Sit down—I'll bring your slippers" and who constantly attended to his needs. Now he was married to an altogether different kind of woman, which required reorientations not only in marital life but also in child rearing. Both were products of their upbringing: my father was a strict disciplinarian, while my mother believed in raising children with respect, gently and lovingly. They struggled to find workable solutions to their disagreements, but the conflicts didn't undermine their love.

Above all, they were drawn to each other's strength of character. My mother wanted a man who, when pushed, would push back instead of yielding passively. My father respected her strength and knew he had outgrown the traditional type of marriage he had shared with Ruth. The time had come for him to break out of the provincial environment of his youth. He was ready for a true partner and ready to emerge into my mother's wider world of travel to faraway places and commitment to a global community. In later years, he often spoke with gratitude of the many ways in which my mother expanded his life.

Both saw in the other a worthy partner, as evidenced by personal strength and a commitment to being true to themselves. They often joked that they both got more than they bargained for, saying, "I wanted someone who was strong, but *this* strong?!" The relationship was solid—and also fiery with conflict.

Before my birth, my family had moved to Fostoria, in northwestern Ohio, where my father worked as the manager of Wood County Packing Company, a slaughterhouse owned by his brother Morris. Early family life centered on my father working hard to support the family while my mother struggled to raise five children and adjust to small-town life. The pervasive atmosphere of McCarthyism during that era heightened my mother's sense of isolation and the pressures to conform.

My mother longed to find work in history, her field of study, but the only available jobs were in teaching, so she decided to take course work to qualify to teach high school. When Rowan, the youngest, was two years old, my mother began classes at Heidelberg College in nearby Findlay, thrilled to have a piece of her life free of children. However, she found the classes uninspiring and decided not to pursue a teaching career.

On February 12, 1960, when I was eight, a fire destroyed the slaughterhouse where my father worked, and our family faced an uncertain future. Weeks later, my father began to experience severe muscle cramps in his legs, arms, and fingers. The cramps lasted from hours to days as his symptoms worsened. Soon his neck and throat became affected, and by April his entire nervous system was involved, with resulting anxiety, restlessness, depression, and inability to concentrate. A Toledo doctor suspected a glandular disorder, but preliminary lab reports didn't substantiate his hunch. In May, my father finally received a diagnosis of primary hypoparathyroidism from specialists at the University of Michigan Hospital in Ann Arbor. By the time he arrived there, his throat and body had become almost rigid.

Primary hypoparathyroidism is a disease in which the parathyroid glands spontaneously stop functioning. The disease is extremely rare (my father's was the sixteenth diagnosed case), but its symptoms are known because of the frequency of accidental damage to the parathyroid glands during thyroid surgery. The primary consequence of the disease is an imbalance of calcium throughout the body. After being treated with massive doses of calcium and vitamin D, my father eventually recovered his health. After the first treatment, he called my mother, elated, proclaiming, "I'm getting better—I'm defrosting!"

By September of that year, precipitated by both the fire and his illness, we moved from Fostoria to Cleveland. My father knew the city from having grown up there, and the business opportunities made it the logical choice. Recovered but shaken, he plunged into new work in the meat business, first as a salesman and then sales manager for Superior Meats, and later in management with Fisher-Fazio-Costa, a large supermarket chain. Burdened by financial responsibility for his large family, he was successful but never secure.

Soon after the move, my mother eagerly accepted a job at Case Western Reserve University researching projects connected with the War on Poverty, including Head Start and Job Corps. Later she was hired by Head Start as a social worker on Cleveland's near west side. She worked part-time to be with her children after school and during summers, continuing as the primary parent even though my father bragged about diapering babies and washing dishes. In the 1960s, she was active in political movements for peace and civil rights. As a family, we marched in demonstrations locally and in Washington, D.C. My mother's respect for human diversity—in language, race, customs, and beliefs—was a dominant thread in my growing up through frequent international guests in our home as well as support for social justice movements around the world.

We lived in University Heights, a middle-class suburb on Cleveland's east side, in a three-story brick home that accommodated our large family and various pets: two cats (Tony the Tiger and Cinder), a drooling basset hound (Doogan—short for Doogan Nogginus Bumpus Tippy Shorty Floppy Silverberg), and a succession of hamsters (Scuttles I, II, III, and IV) that kept escaping their cage and dying inside our basement walls. Our home was modestly furnished in keeping with our casual lifestyle— Swedish modern furniture, turkey-red Pirotski rugs brought by my mother from Yugoslavia, copper trays and bowls from the Middle East, earthenware pottery, and throw pillows embroidered with folk designs. We didn't fit in with, or aspire to join, our upwardly mobile neighbors who covered their sofas in plastic and shopped for name-brand clothing at Cleveland's fancy department stores—Sterling-Lindner, Halle's, Best and Company. My father declined the offer of a Cadillac from his employer, eschewing the status connotations, and instead asked for a large station wagon.

Our affiliation with Judaism was cultural rather than religious. We enjoyed Jewish humor, blintzes, and noodle kugel, and like many other Jews we valued education, activism, and cultural enrichment. Although my parents' spiritual leanings were humanistic, they sent us to Sunday school through confirmation at age fourteen to expose us to our religious roots so that as adults we could each make an informed choice about our beliefs.

We picnicked in city parks for Sunday breakfast and studied drawing at the art museum. Music—lessons, concerts, and chamber music gatherings at home—played a prominent role in our family life. My parents, tired of small-town living, reveled in Cleveland's cultural scene, particularly the concerts, plays, and movies.

Family priorities included vacations—to Manitoulin Island in Lake Huron, Deer Isle in Maine, and cottages along Lake Erie—as well as educational camps for a child's special interest. Kathie studied violin at Interlochen National Music Camp, and Rowan and I attended summer programs (hers in Denver and mine in Great Falls, Montana) that brought together teens from varied backgrounds to build community and learn about active citizenship. During college years, Mark lived on an Israeli kibbutz for a semester, and I attended a French immersion summer program in Montreal.

CHAPTER 4

Growing Up with My Father

I was born in 1951, when my father was thirty-five and my mother was thirty-two. When I was one week old, a practical nurse staying with us discovered that I was having trouble breathing and had started to turn blue. As she rushed me outside to go to the hospital, the cold air apparently triggered my lungs to begin working again. Tests turned up nothing treatable and no clue as to the cause of my breathing problem.

In part because of this close call, I was raised as a fragile child in need of protection and sheltering. Temperamentally more sensitive than my siblings, I was also shy, especially around strangers. My mother, who called me a "scared little rabbit," felt that it was her mission to make the world safe for me. When I was young, she respected my introverted nature and didn't force me to be sociable with visitors or in public settings like summer camp and large gatherings. But she overprotected and overcomforted at every turn, which I believe reinforced and exaggerated my sensitive temperament. Many times I've watched her treat young children in the same way; at the slightest hint of frustration or upset, she encircles them with her arms, rocks them gently, and assures them that everything will be okay, failing to see that everything already *is* okay. By intervening to comfort me before I sought comfort, she interrupted my natural ability to process emotions and blocked the opportunity for me to learn to recenter myself or ask for comfort when needed.

For just this reason, I grew up lacking the ability to comfort myself. I ached for comfort from outside but rarely found solace other than from my stuffed animals. When I try to conjure up memories of childhood comfort, I recall my mother holding me too tightly and a visceral need to break free. I don't know whether she overcomforted because of my near-death, her need to be needed, or a drive to enact comfort for scared parts of herself. I do know that it contributed to an overarching need for space and independence that has guided my choices to be child-free and pet-free, to live alone for decades, and to limit my entanglements with other people. A true introvert, I generally experience contact with others as more draining than nourishing.

In recent years I've come to better understand my temperament thanks to Dr. Elaine Aron's research on the trait of high sensitivity. Highly sensitive people, who make up about one-fifth of the population, have a different type of nervous system and therefore process sensory data differently. High sensitivity is well within the normal range of human variation and is thought to confer certain survival advantages, including a heightened awareness of subtleties in one's surroundings, as well as certain challenges, such as the potential to become overstimulated by crowds, loud music, clutter, and other situations. The trait has been mistakenly confused with shyness, social anxiety, fearfulness, and fragility, all of which may manifest in stressful settings but which are not innate qualities of the trait. In my family, my sensitivity was largely seen as a defect, and my mother went into overdrive trying to be my savior.

My father, on the other hand, agonized over my perceived frailty and felt helpless to make me stronger. In his discomfort, he distanced himself from me, leaving the caretaking to my mother.

My mother's comfort, though gentle and kind, usually had a clutching quality to it. She is an extrovert who thrives on contact with others, but beneath her sociable exterior lies a deep need for validation from others. I always sensed that she wanted more from me than I wanted to give. Over time, she tried to lure me out of hiding, claiming it was for my own good—she agonized about how I'd find a place in the world if I stuck to myself—but in retrospect I believe it was more about her needs than mine. If she could "cure" me, it would validate her own style and make her the "good parent" who knew how to reach even a scared rabbit like me. When I was eight and we moved to Cleveland, she began coaxing me to be more social and outgoing. She gave me little pep talks to try to shore up my confidence, not realizing that the core problem wasn't a lack of self-esteem—it was a feeling of unsafety that no amount of socializing could remedy. The problem wasn't within me—it was in my interface with the world and my pervasive experience of not being received as I was by others, which her parenting style only compounded.

So I grew up experiencing one parent as invasive and the other as rejecting. Added to this were my father's violence, threats, and criticism—a different type of invasion. As a result, I longed for both more space and more closeness and was left unsatisfied by every variety of interaction that came my way. The closeness was intrusive and smothering, and the space was shunning and abandoning.

My relationship with my father was complicated from early on. He was my superhero; as a child I idealized him, as did my siblings. Mark bragged to his elementary school classmates that our six-foot-three father was a giant. One day when Dad visited Mark's school to drop off a permission slip, Mark proclaimed to his classmates, "See, I *told* you he's a giant!" In addition to being physically imposing, he filled a room with his charisma and intensity. His clowning, comedic timing, and musical and acting talents would have served him well in vaudeville.

I idealized him as well simply because he was my father. It never would have occurred to me to see him as flawed or wrong—grouchy, perhaps, but not wrong. I lacked the psychological maturity to hold my discrepant experiences of him as "adored Daddy" and "violent Daddy." Yet neither could I ignore my terror of his volatility. Many times he turned on Mark, Rowan, or me with no warning.

One evening when I was seven, my father was playing chamber music in the living room with several friends. Up past my bedtime, I was mesmerized by the music and the passionate energy of the musicians. After two of the men left, my father and the cellist, a close family friend named Frank, were talking and laughing expansively. I joined in, reveling in the opportunity to share a joyful moment with adults. Without warning, my father erupted in rage. He lunged at me, grabbed me roughly by the shoulders, and threw me out into the hall, yelling, "GET IN BED—RIGHT NOW!" This kind of turn-on-a-dime mood change was typical. As a child, I felt as though my father could morph into a monster and attack me at any minute.

Most of my siblings' and my transgressions were minor—not washing dinner dishes immediately, playing or watching television instead of doing our homework, bickering on road trips. My father is the original author of the line "Don't make me stop the car." I was so anxious on road trips that I perfected the art of carsickness. I usually had time to ask my father to pull over to the shoulder, but once on a trip from Fostoria to Toledo, I threw up all over the inside of his brother Morris's brand-new Cadillac. Rowan's specialty was spilling her milk at the dinner table.

We weren't bad kids, we were just *kids*—expected by our father to be much more self-disciplined than we were capable of being. Many times we didn't even know what had upset him, only that he could go from calm to crazed in an instant. We became expert at reading the subtle indicators of his rage: a glare, a tight jaw, an arm tensed to strike. From both actual violence and the threat of it, we learned to behave, keep silent, and do everything in our power to avoid making Daddy angry.

The fierceness that made my father such a terror to live with also fueled his deep sense of justice. He loved a good fight—in part because he relished being right and teaching people a lesson, but also because he welcomed the challenge of standing up for his beliefs. He was dedicated to equality and outspoken in its defense.

When we lived in Fostoria in the early 1950s, my father sought a secretary for Wood County Packing Company. Among the qualified applicants was an African American woman named Lois Burch, whom he hired. There were no African American secretaries in Fostoria at the time; his decision was precedent setting in an era when segregation was the norm. He didn't care what anyone thought—he simply hired the best person for the job.

In Fostoria, ours was one of only fifteen Jewish families in a town of fourteen thousand. My parents felt strongly that we children should not attend the religious education classes that were a regular feature of public school, both on Constitutional grounds (separation of church and state) and because it wasn't religious education (education about the world's religions)—it was Protestant education, which wasn't our religious tradition. We became accustomed to sitting in the school hallway during those classes.

One day Mark came home from school and announced that the evening parent visitation was going to include religious education class. My father immediately called the superintendent of schools to inform him that if the class were held as scheduled, my father would take him to court the next morning. Lo and behold, at Parents' Night my mother and father learned about geography and history. Many years later, the school superintendent told my mother that my father's stand had profoundly affected his understanding of the rights of minorities.

(My father investigated the possibility of challenging the board of education with a court case, but he was advised by the Anti-Defamation League—an arm of the Jewish humanitarian, human rights, and advocacy organization B'nai Brith that fights discrimination—that it would be more effective if a non-Jew challenged the practice of religious education in public schools.)

~

We moved from Fostoria to Cleveland in August 1960, a few months before I turned nine. My father's recent recovery from primary hypoparathyroidism and his concerns about supporting his family exacerbated the stresses on our large family starting fresh in a new city. Leaving behind a spacious ranch home on a rural half-acre lot for a three-story brick house in a crowded Cleveland suburb added to the difficulty of the move.

When we moved to the new home, my father gave the walls in the living room and up the staircase a fresh coat of white paint. Rowan, who had just turned four, perceived this bright expanse as an inviting canvas for artistic creation. Lost in gleeful reverie, she applied her crayons to it. Our father came up behind her with no warning and hit her—hard—across the back. Wailing, she ran upstairs and hid under her bed. He yelled up the stairs, "If you cry more, I'll hit you more."

I vaguely remember him striking her and her anguished scream. But I still feel his fury in my cells, as if he were still alive and in the next room. And I remember thinking, for the thousandth time, that my father was a monster and wondering how I'd survive my childhood living in the same house with him.

That question stayed with me as I began fourth grade at Northwood Elementary School. I had no awareness of social hierarchy and was quickly brought up short after developing a crush on

Tony Riccardo, the cutest boy in school. He made it clear—to me as well as to all my classmates—that he didn't hang out with nerdy girls like me. I was a pariah just weeks after starting at my new school, and family life was worse still. I dreaded my father's temper even more than being teased and shunned at school.

That fall I ran away from home. Actually, "ran away" isn't quite accurate—I just didn't go home after school one day. I sat on a swing at the school playground, unable to bring myself to walk the six blocks home and face my family. Martha, a neighbor girl who was in junior high, happened to come by the playground, and we talked about my desire to run away. I suspect that she alerted my family to my whereabouts. When my father drove up to retrieve me, the sun was already low in the sky. My parents were relieved that I was safe, but I despaired that my few hours of freedom had ended.

My father encouraged us children to praise him and regularly asked, "Who's the greatest?" The appropriate response, of course, was, "You are, Dad." He often directed us to recite, "My daddy can do everything." At the time, I had no doubt that he really *could* do everything. I believed whatever he wanted me to believe because he held all the power and because, at that age, I needed someone to idealize. Never mind that I lived in constant fear of him—he was still my daddy, my hero. Any evidence to the contrary was neatly stuffed into a dark place that holds feelings too painful to acknowledge. On the back of a school photo from that era, I wrote, "Dear Big Louie, You're the greatest, as you already know. Really—you're a wonderful father, besides being perfect in every way! You can do everything!"

At age eleven, I woke up to the fact that he wasn't omnipotent. My realization might have been connected with something that happened one night while my parents were out and a friend of my father's was visiting from New York City. My father played up Leon as another magical, larger-than-life figure: he jumped over creeks, he took us for rides in his sports car, he wore flaming red ascots. One evening in the family room, Leon invited me to sit on his knee, reached under my blouse and bra, and fondled my breasts. Moments later he slipped his hand down my pants, gently pulled aside the crotch of my underpants, and inserted a finger into my vagina. I was so naive at the time that I didn't understand what he was doing. In retrospect, I also believe that my father's abuse, and perhaps my mother's restrictive holding as well, had so conditioned me to believe that my body wasn't my own that I didn't experience Leon's actions as boundary violations. I had no conscious awareness that anything wrong was taking place, so it never occurred to me to get off his lap or tell him to stop, let alone to feel outraged by his actions. I was also so starved for attention from a father figure that I didn't know how to discriminate between healthy and unhealthy varieties.

Soon after the Leon incident, I mustered the courage to confront my father for the first time. We were in the living room when he launched into a tirade about everything I was doing wrong: leaving my junk on the stairs, tracking in dirt from outside, wearing sloppy clothes, scowling instead of sporting a happy face. Something inside snapped—I'd had it with being verbally and emotionally beaten up every time we were in the same room. I blurted out, "You *can't* do everything after all. You sure can't stop picking on me."

That moment was his fall from the pedestal, and it freed me from the bondage of a Disney worldview where the birds are always singing and no one has authentic feelings. My father had the good sense to know that this fall was positive and important. Right up to the time of his death, he continued to tell the story of how I "let him have it" and that he was tempted to "knock me on my ass" but resisted because he knew how crucial it was for me to find my voice and my power. He rarely was able to remember that wisdom in later confrontations, but I remain grateful to him for not flattening me the first time I tested my wings.

During my early teens, I was inwardly hostile and resentful of my father's unreasonable restrictions on my life. Internally I had broken free from blind obedience, but rather than fight for my rights, I withdrew and did everything in my power to avoid him. I was an extreme loner, shunning contact with most people and preferring to hole up in my room with a book or an art project.

My isolation was in part a defense against the hurt I felt when he distanced himself from me. I have vague memories of him being physically nurturing when I was a young child—hugging me and allowing me to sit on his lap, where I felt protected in the circle of his strong arms and warm chest. He became much more distant around the time the abuse began when I was seven or eight, which roughly coincided with the fire at Wood County Packing Company and the onset of his hypoparathyroidism, when his stress levels skyrocketed. He withdrew all physical nurturance by the time I entered puberty; my mother later told me that he presumed physical closeness between a father and daughter to be unsafe. His withdrawal left me feeling abandoned and confused. I believed it was my fault and felt untouchable, thinking that others also perceived my emerging womanhood as toxic. I became even more introverted, unable to tolerate any physical contact.

My father had the strange habit of pinching his children on the butt. It wasn't sexual or overtly hostile—rather, a "gotcha" thing. One of the games he played with us was to ask, "Inch-me and Pinch-me went down to the lake. Inch-me fell in. Who was left?" If we said, "Pinch-me," he would, of course, pinch us. If we didn't say it, he would chase us with pinching fingers. When I asked him in later years why he pinched us, he said, "I wanted you to grow up comfortable with being touched, to prepare you for healthy adulthood." How strange to try to teach physicality with a touch guaranteed to cause flinching. Coupled with the hitting and physical threats, I definitely didn't grow up comfortable with being touched—quite the opposite.

～

In the spring of 1966, when I was fourteen, my parents bought twenty-nine acres of land in Ashtabula County, an hour east of Cleveland, with their good friends Chuck and Milly. Our family felt constricted by our suburban neighborhood with houses one narrow driveway apart and the continual unwelcome exposure to the neighbors' dramas. Close to fifty years later, I can still hear Cyril, our neighbor to the south, calling, "FRED-dee!" to her husband in a whiny, grating voice. We desperately needed an escape.

The land was located in a private valley bounded by steep hills and dense woods on two adjacent sides, with a road and covered bridge near the entrance. The fourth side was a branch of the Ashtabula River that became our comfort and refuge. The center of the land, a huge meadow perfect for badminton and stargazing, was the site of a large vegetable garden in later years.

Chuck and Milly and my parents each had their own residence for weekend visits. My family's, an old picnic shelter we referred to as "the red building" and later as *Vikendica* (Serbo-Croatian for "weekend place"), was a 750-square-foot shack made of ill-fitting wooden planks, equipped with electricity but no running water. Red squirrels nested in the eaves, and bugs entered at will. A pot-bellied stove occupied the center of the linoleum-tiled main room, which contained cast-off furniture gathered from our Cleveland basement or donated by relatives and friends. A small corner room provided a storage area as well as privacy for changing clothes.

On Saturday mornings we fled Cleveland for two days, packing jeans and T-shirts, beat-up sneakers newly designated as river shoes, five-gallon jugs of water, expensive steaks (a perk of my father's work in the meat business), salad fixings, potato salad, and "terrible cake" (a divine mix of chocolate, dates, and walnuts, so named because it's terribly hard to stop eating). Each trip began with my father exploding in anger. We dawdled too much while getting ready, we messed up his perfect design for loading the car, we disrupted the Master Plan. He expected all of us, my mother included, to yield to his authority and accommodate his impatience to get out of Cleveland.

The 1960s were stressful times for our family. My father worked at first as a salesman for Superior Meats, home of Frankie the Keener Weiner, selling to supermarket chains around northern Ohio. My mother recalled that he would "bust his ass" on the road month after month, terrified that he wouldn't earn adequate commissions to support his family. By the time Saturday morning rolled around, he was a live wire, desperate for relief from a stressful week but unable to relax. Throwing a fit during the transition was a predictable ritual. By the time we were on the road for the hour-long drive to the valley, the prospect of two days trapped in a tiny shack with my father left me feeling like a convict frantic to escape my cell.

Fortunately, escape was abundantly available in the valley. I spent many days walking downstream along the edge of the river, looking for snakes and neat rocks. Or I'd venture deep into the woods and discover a huge patch of bluebells midway in their transition from pale pink to blue. But my greatest comfort during those years came from time spent with the Ellsworths, our neighbors up the road.

The Ellsworths had a daughter my age, Mary, with whom I quickly became friends. Their barn housed Babo, the fattest pony on earth, and Pancho, a burro who enjoyed countywide fame for horse show ribbons under the tutelage of Mary's younger sister,

Janet. After Mary taught me to ride, I became so enthralled that my family eventually acquired two horses, Robb and Boomer, which we boarded with the Ellsworths. Robb was a brown quarter horse given to my father by a business associate. When it became clear that the Ellsworths could accommodate another horse, the same man gave my father Boomer, an enormous old chestnut.

Mary and I appropriated Robb and Boomer for our weekend riding, leaving Babo and Pancho to Rowan and Janet. Boomer was an exquisitely gentle horse despite his huge size (seventeen hands). On his back I really learned to ride—to meld with his powerful energy and guide him using my newly discovered body intuition. The safety of my connection with Boomer eased my hypervigilance and provided me with a kinesthetic experience of trust that counteracted the all-too-familiar climate of abuse and fear. Whereas my father would turn on me with no warning, Boomer was constant, loyal, and kind. He honored my need for gentleness without compromising his strength, and in doing so not only served as my surrogate father during those years but also provided me with a template for intimacy that continues to serve me well. I learned from Boomer that strength and gentleness, far from being polar opposites, are a wonderful blend.

Those weekends in the valley offered me windows onto life outside the tyranny of my father's rage, and even more important, onto who I was apart from my adaptations to his rage. I was still a very messed-up teenager whose outlook on life had been seriously distorted by my upbringing, as evidenced by my motto during high school: *Life is a shit sandwich, and every day you take another bite.* Yet racing across a country field on Boomer or riding him along the river's edge planted seeds of hope in me. Maybe life wouldn't always be so hard. Maybe I wouldn't always feel so alone and misunderstood. Boomer honored my tender nature—not in an infantilizing way, as did my mother, who seemed to equate sensitivity with fragility—and my wildness finally found a safe place for expression. Being with Boomer was my first taste of wholeness. Those weekends also provided me with a different experience of my father. In Cleveland, consumed by the daily grind of long, stressful workdays, he came home every evening desperate for a shred of peace before repeating the routine the next day. In the valley, his edginess let up to some extent, and I began to see a side of him I had only seen before on summer vacations.

Two long stone slabs in the river formed a large bathtub-shaped area we called "the whirlpool." A slate outcropping on the near edge provided a perfect picnic spot, replete with the steady purr of rushing water. My father often suggested a visit to the whirl-pool for a cheese-and-crackers picnic. He began to unwind at the river's edge, and the valley's healing effect on him was palpable. (My parents usually brought along gin and tonics or a couple of cans of Miller, which I'm certain played a role in his expansive-ness.)

My father delighted in the nature around him and was often the first to notice a pool of tadpoles or a new hatchling in a red-tailed hawk's nest. He also noticed trees that had fallen or been carried downstream. After dragging them to the meadow with the Ellsworths' tractor, he cut them up with his trusty chain saw and stacked the wood for fuel. We teased him affectionately about his Daniel Boone persona because he took such pleasure in being a woodsman. He was an expert fire builder, first with the potbellied stove and at our bonfire circle, and later in the fireplace crafted from river stones in the dream home he and my mother built in the valley after Rowan left for college in 1974. Caring for the tangible needs of life in the country grounded him in his physical-ity and provided regular outlets for his intense energy. When he was frustrated, he could rip through a dead maple with his chain saw instead of ripping through his kids. And whereas in Cleveland he had only a weekly paycheck to show for his hard work, in the valley he had a stack of firewood and later a bountiful garden over which he proudly presided.

During those years I didn't comprehend that the valley was slowly softening my father, changing him as surely as the river currents were smoothing the edges of stones. Those are the stories of *his* transformation, preserved by my mother since his passing. I only knew that weekends in the valley sometimes offered family times free of anger, conflict, and the threat of violence. On winter evenings, we gathered around the potbellied stove drinking hot chocolate and playing music—my father on violin, Rowan on flute, I on guitar. On steamy summer afternoons, we frolicked in the swimming hole under the covered bridge and savored just-picked raspberries with fresh cream from neighbors up the road.

Still, back in Cleveland during the week, my father generally reverted to the rageaholic I was conditioned to expect. When my best friend, Janis, came over after school and stayed for dinner, my father would strictly control conversations so that no silliness erupted. Janis, who was the Queen of Silliness, thought my father was a tyrant. Before long, Janis and I made a point of hanging out at her house instead of mine. I welcomed the weekday escapes from my father's rages and control tactics. Janis's parents were mellower, even if they did insult her regularly; Janis is one of the most ambition-deficient people I've ever known, and her parents had an uncanny knack for finding opportunities to tell her she was lazy and would never amount to much. (Ironically, the money she inherited when they died has allowed her to live job-free for decades.) During high school years, Janis and I spent an inordinate amount of time drinking Diet-Rite Cola and playing cards—bid whist was our favorite—with her parents. It wasn't the culturally rich or politically savvy environment of my own home, but it was peaceful, and the reprieve from my father's temper was heavenly.

After more than ten years of praying daily for release from life under the tyranny of my father's rule, I went to college in the fall of 1969—to Oakland University, near Pontiac, Michigan—and was finally free of my parents' strictures. I gained twenty pounds, indiscriminately eating pasta, bread, French fries, Hostess berry pies, and soft-serve ice cream smuggled out of the campus cafeteria. I smoked cigarettes—a pack a day or more—as well as marijuana or hashish at least twice a day and experimented with hallucinogens on weekends. And I started stealing.

I can still feel in my body the thrill I got from stealing. Even more than drugs, stealing allowed me to express a rebellious energy that was forbidden in my family. I was supposed to be high achieving, politically aware, and, of course, obedient—or, more accurately, obedient within my family but a feisty activist out in the world. I was allowed to get angry about the Vietnam War but expected to keep silent about my father's dictatorial behavior. My parents regularly told my siblings and me that we were lucky to grow up in such a wonderful family.

My rebellious side—a natural outgrowth of the pressure to be overly compliant when I was young—desperately needed an outlet, and I found a good one. I stole matching T-shirts for ten friends and persuaded everyone to wear them on the same day in a group proclamation of defiance. I stole jewelry, office supplies, groceries. I found a key to a vending machine and stole snacks for months until the lock was changed. I stole for the thrill of feeling my own power and to tell the world: *No one can control me. I can get away with anything I want.*

I got caught once, in a grocery store. The manager took me to a back room and said, "You know, I could have you arrested for this." I pleaded tearfully that he not go to that extreme, saying my parents would pull me out of college. (I was crying real tears at the prospect of being back in the prison of my father's home as well as the prospect of my parents discovering I wasn't such a good girl after all.) The manager decided instead to have me write a letter to my parents recounting the theft and promising never again to steal. I wrote a letter and addressed the envelope to my sister Deedee and her then-husband, lying that the last name was different because my mother had remarried. The manager never sent the letter.

Eventually I did stop stealing, but not because it was wrong. As I learned to be assertive and started claiming agency in my life in less covert ways, my need to steal fell away. Autonomous power, when denied to a child, will go underground, but it *will* find a way out. I consider that a good thing—an indication that the spirit isn't completely broken. The solution isn't to forcefully extinguish delinquent behaviors but rather to find healthier outlets for power and wildness.

Becoming assertive and finding my power began in earnest during the summer after my freshman year in college. While I was growing up, my sensitive self was on the surface and my fierce self was in hiding. When the shift occurred, those two selves swapped places; I became outspoken and fearless, with vulnerable feelings now banished to unconsciousness. Family members, baffled by the switch, were clearly uncomfortable when I disrupted habitual patterns of relating. My newfound assertiveness prompted my brother's reproach, still uttered on occasion, "Go back in your shell."

This assertiveness carried into my relationship with my father. I was definitely no longer a scared little rabbit who cowered in fear of his anger. One evening during a visit home from college when he issued an order for immediate quiet, I blurted out angrily, "You know, you're not the only one who lives here." When a shouting match followed, I left the table screaming that he was a dictator. When he lectured me for dropping a class or for not getting straight As, I called him authoritarian and told him he couldn't run my life. Each time he issued an order, I countered with blaming criticism. I didn't see then that my angry style matched his— that I had become hardened and rageful just like the person I so vehemently opposed. I only knew I would no longer passively stand by and allow him to rule my life.

Reclaiming my anger and my right to have it was enormously healing for me, after growing up in a family in which everyone's behavior constellated around my father. He was the only one allowed to be angry; everyone else had to be silent, accommodating, and well behaved. I felt continual pressure to tone myself down and be less intense. We all felt anger, of course—we just found ways to stuff it. For example, my siblings and I have all struggled with compulsive overeating at various times in our lives.

During my college years, my parents traveled to Yugoslavia, where my mother had worked after World War II. They took Rowan and met Mark there following his semester in Israel. They invited me to join them, but I declined because I knew that when I returned, I'd have to spend the rest of the summer cashiering at Fazio's, a supermarket that was part of the chain where my father now worked as a vice president. (We were dubiously honored with regular visits from the Oscar Meyer Wienermobile, a huge hot-dog-shaped vehicle whose driver, a little person, would pass out mauve plastic wiener-shaped whistles to all the kids in the neighborhood. After each visit, the irritating, high-pitched blasts echoed up and down our block for weeks.) When I was sixteen, my father had set me up with a part-time cashiering job that I returned to during summer breaks from college. The work was deadly boring and painful as well, since I had inherited his severely flat feet and had trouble standing in one place all day. I wasn't about to spend another summer at Fazio's, so I opted for a job as a camp counselor and skipped the trip to Yugoslavia. The next offer to accompany my parents to Europe came when I was twenty-six and living in Cleveland, just months after a hard breakup with Dominic, my first love. I seized the opportunity.

Europe was heaven—the museums of Florence, the pristine beaches of Croatia, leisurely days with a family friend on Lošinj, a small island in the Adriatic. But the family dynamics were as familiar as an old T-shirt: my father was the boss and decision maker, and my mother and I were expected to comply. If she and I wanted to go to a shop, cafe, or art gallery and he didn't, he would veto the idea, and that was that. If we started discussing something he didn't want to talk about, especially anything introspective or conflictual, he would change the subject or sharply say *dosta* (Serbo-Croatian for "enough").

My mother was more willing than I to be silent in the interest of avoiding conflict. Many times each day when we faced choices about restaurants, museums, or shopping, he'd insist on making the decisions, and I'd say, "You know, you're not the only one here." He didn't take kindly to having his authority challenged. By the end of the three-week trip, I was primed to move cross-country, which I did eight months later, to Las Cruces, New Mexico, thrilled to be far from my father. Although I was grateful for my parents' generosity and my first taste of overseas travel, the trip confirmed that being with my father was tense and trying at best, and a volatile power struggle at worst. (My mother believed that the dynamic of having an extra person present threw their habitual travel mode out of balance; she claimed that they traveled much more peacefully when alone.)

My relationship with my father was dominated by conflict, but as I became an adult we shared pockets of joyful time together, often when his customary defenses weren't operating thanks to either sleep deprivation or a bit of alcohol. When my parents and I were delayed at the Trieste, Italy, train station for five hours in a state of great fatigue, my father and I worked on a crossword puzzle to pass the time. After filling in the words we knew, we were left with several empty squares. My father, acting as though he'd just had a Nobel Prize-winning thought, filled in the blanks with letters that created nonsense words, which propelled both of us into an uncontrollable fit of giggling.

One of my treasured memories of my father is from a wedding I attended with him and my mother. He'd been asked to play the *Fiddler on the Roof* song "Sunrise, Sunset" on his violin during the ceremony. Stage fright prompted him to bring along a flask of whiskey to bolster his courage. Before long, he was considerably "happier" than I'd ever seen him. As he, my mother, and I sat among the attendees waiting for his performance cue, he started cutting up with me, making faces like a mischievous schoolboy who'd been told to sit still and behave. He and I ended up with a terrific case of the giggles, which prompted my mother to give us the look our family calls the "hairy eyeball." Each time she did so and then turned back to watch the ceremony, he imitated her as though mocking her authority, which triggered another round of raucous, out-of-control laughter in the two of us. It's a miracle he managed to get through his performance without a hitch, and another miracle that he and I weren't asked to leave. Although interactions such as those didn't mend the rift between us, they allowed us to step outside our habitual conflicts and share moments of playfulness and joy.

Over the years, I attempted to communicate without blame and rage, yet I still struggled to find ways to converse with my father. He wasn't a man who liked to talk things out, although he became slightly more approachable in later years. I always felt as though I only got fifty words to present my entire "case," and if I didn't use his language and follow his rules, he'd either lose attention or shut down in anger.

I tried to talk with him about my decision to move from Las Cruces to Ithaca, New York. My job at New Mexico State University had become untenable due to a new department head, and I was working four part-time jobs to make ends meet. My sister Rowan was living in Philadelphia at the time, and we decided to move to Ithaca to be together as well as to live in a progressive college town. When I told my father I was moving, his only question was, "Do you have a job lined up?"

"No, but it'll work out," I replied.

His eyes got steely, his jaw tightened, and he barked, "I think you're making a big mistake. You should be saving for your retirement, not starting from scratch in a new city."

But my life wasn't guided by security—it was guided by internal promptings that I was committed to heeding, with trust in the Universe as my companion. Two weeks after moving, I saw an ad for a managerial position at a print shop and knew at once it was my job. I worked there for six years, and although my father came around to being supportive, his initial reaction ground into me a sense that whatever my choices, I could count on him to criticize.

Even decisions of lesser import, such as taking up the banjo or vacationing in Scotland for several years in a row, met with criticism. Attempts to connect and share my life with him were doomed from the start, and I was furious that our relationship always had to be on his terms. Our communications cycled between explosive conflicts, uneasy truces with unresolvable issues carefully sidestepped, fragile attempts to be peaceful together, and occasional extended periods without contact.

Emotionally, my father seemed to operate at survival level, always guarding the gate lest the wolves get in and devour him. As an adult, I've come to understand this aspect of him and to feel compassion for the poverty and abuse that molded his volatile personality. He learned violence and fear with his ABCs and never found a way to heal from those early terrors. He wasn't violent by nature—simply a child who suffered at the hands of an out-of-control father who didn't know the bounds of normal discipline, even for those times. As a child, my father never learned the difference between discipline and violence, and therefore could not distinguish those two forces in himself.

Additionally, he was raised in a culture that didn't cherish children as unique souls deserving of attentive nurturing, a culture that not only condoned but mandated physical punishment for successful child rearing. He also lived during an era when self-inquiry and psychological healing were neither accessible nor considered effective ways to solve problems. He lacked the tools to heal darker aspects of his psyche and was entirely at their effect when they were triggered. Like his father, he morphed into a violent tyrant driven to stamp out chaos, disobedience, and imperfection.

Difficult events in my father's own life exacerbated his temper. While writing this book, I learned details from my mother of the terrible stress he experienced when Wood County Packing Company burned down, when he was ill with undiagnosed hypoparathyroidism, and when, after we moved to Cleveland in 1960, he struggled to support a wife and five children on $100 a week plus commissions. Those challenges would have pushed to the limit the coping skills of someone with good tools for managing stress. In the absence of tools, my father's anger took the path of least resistance—trying to manage his chaotic world by silencing and controlling his young children.

My work to heal from my childhood doesn't replace painful realities with Little Mary Sunshine smiles or "forgive and forget" slogans. Healing allows me to hold the pain—both my father's and my own—tenderly and compassionately. I can view his life and travails with empathy and love, and also bring that empathy to my own life. I can feel for my father's pain and also state squarely that his failings wreaked havoc on my childhood. His rage, violence, and lack of support all injured me profoundly.

The two things that have been the most painful in my relationship with my father—living in constant fear of his anger and not being acknowledged as good or lovable—clearly stem from his childhood. When he was young, his mother—the person he most adored and with whom he felt safest—never told him she loved him. Now I see why he never affirmed me in that way. I'd come home from school with an almost-perfect report card, longing to hear "That's wonderful!" Instead, his response was, "Can't you do any better?" with a little smirk. I couldn't have known at the time that underneath his response was the superstitious belief *We can't call attention to this blessing or it'll be taken away.* Instead I heard the message that no matter how well I did, I was never good enough for my father.

CHAPTER 5

My Mother's Role

Few images come when I try to see my mother through the eyes of my early childhood. In my earliest vivid memory of her, I'm looking up from the tailgate of our family's station wagon to her fourth-floor hospital room, waving to her soon after Rowan was born. I was almost five by then, and thousands of interactions had occurred between us before that point, but I only remember a vague sense of comfort overlaid by a feeling of being smothered by her. Now when I think about those early years, most of what comes to mind is the phrase *I need more room to breathe* and a compelling urge to escape her clutches.

I didn't start to remember until well into adulthood the feeling of being smothered by her. At age forty in a guided imagery session, I saw myself as an infant wrapped in a pale yellow baby blanket with pinstripes of red, blue, green, and white. When I asked my mother if a real blanket like that had existed, she answered that yes, there had been one just like that. I still have body memories of being held in that blanket, always accompanied by the feeling of being held too tight, unable to move.

I imagine that as an infant, I was already developing a compliant, accommodating facade—staying still and silent, enduring what was imposed on me rather than making my needs known. I imagine that any restlessness as an infant was taken for discomfort, which would have made my mother hold me even closer, trying to soothe me with her constant presence, when what I wanted instead was space. But how can a baby want that? How can an infant long for anything other than the healing arms of its mother? Or so I imagine my mother thought. In addition to being repelled by her smothering, I believe I already had a physical craving for room to breathe from my near-fatal breathing crisis as a newborn.

I also may have been born with that craving. My mother was overwhelmed by her life before I came along. In under two years, she married my father, acquired two instant daughters, gave birth to my brother, almost died from an allergic reaction to penicillin, lost her mother suddenly to a stroke, struggled alone weekdays with three children while my father explored the possibility of moving to Fostoria, and then found out she was pregnant with me. She was already at her limit, and the prospect of another child at that point was devastating. Although she and my father reconciled themselves to my impending birth and eventually came around to eager anticipation, I'm certain that on some level I absorbed her ambivalence and felt unwelcome. I imagine that even while in her womb, I was thinking, *Let me out of here!* My need for space and privacy is so dominant a theme in my life that I suspect it has been present from birth or earlier.

Eight months after I was born, my mother's back gave out—the physical equivalent of a nervous breakdown. Mark and I went to live with Aunt Rose, our father's sister, for a month. When our parents came to retrieve us, the story goes, I clung to Aunt Rose and refused to go to my mother's arms.

Growing up, I experienced my mother as the "good parent" and my father as the "bad parent." My father was an easier target for my anger because he was unapproachable and critical as well as violent. My mother was much more accommodating—we always went to Amy Joy Donuts after a trip to the dentist—and kinder when she had to say no. Children latch onto their best hope for safety, and my mother was mine. She was the parent I sought out when I was upset since she was less reactive and far more reasonable and supportive. In truth, she was not so much the "safe parent" as the "less unsafe parent." Because I relied on her so heavily, the conflicting desire to escape her clutches went underground.

As a consequence, my idealization of my mother lasted quite a bit longer than my idealization of my father. By the time I reached adolescence, my father was number one on my "shit list," whereas I didn't begin to see through the unconscious patterns in my relationship with my mother until my forties. The day after I first questioned that relationship in a therapy session with Paul, I had a panic attack while driving in freeway traffic. I had no inkling of how severely my psychological stability would be disrupted by examining her role in my life.

While studying psychology in graduate school, I learned about family systems theory and began to see my family in a new light. I came to see my father in the classic "abuser" role, the one around whose behavior other family members constellated. My mother, despite her activism and social conscience, in many ways fit the role of the "enabler"—the one who, by not confronting problems head-on, gave her tacit consent and allowed them to continue.

Her role as stepmother to Deedee and Kathie was a key ingredient in this pattern. When my mother joined the family six months after Ruth's death, she was determined to provide the girls with as much nurturing as possible. In the following two years, Mark and I were born, and my mother found herself transformed from a free spirit working and traveling on two continents to a wife and mother of four living in a small town in Ohio. She was overwhelmed by the challenges she faced in everyday living—four needy children ages seven and under, the house a perpetual mess, and a demanding husband who was accustomed to a traditional wife. When Rowan joined us five years later, my mother's responsibilities again increased. Adding to her stress over the years was the anguish of watching her husband discipline us younger children with anger, violence, and little regard for our humanity. (My father was rarely abusive to the older girls, having become their protector after their biological mother died.)

Several years after my father's death, I told my mother about the work I was doing in therapy to heal the terror that still lived in my body from my father's violence. I asked if she had ever considered leaving. At first she said, "I had no idea it would have such a serious impact on you." After a moment, she added, "Deedee and Kathie lost one mother, and I couldn't cause them to lose a second one."

As I absorbed that information, a wave of anger rose in me. I was angry that she chose Deedee's and Kathie's welfare over the welfare of us younger children—a choice she could only have made by not acknowledging the harm done to us by being raised in a violent environment. I was also angry that she relinquished power in her marriage by choosing to stay no matter what happened.

What did I learn as a result of her choice? I learned that my mother was not nearly as strong or principled as she claimed to be. I learned that men stick to their guns and women back off, choosing love over principles, harmony over integrity. I learned that women sacrifice their needs—and their children—to preserve a marriage.

As a young girl, I was confused about my mother's role as a woman. I was proud of her commitment to social justice and activism. I liked that she'd been a free spirit until the age of thirty. I knew she wasn't a "yes, dear" type of wife, at least on the surface. Countless times I saw her speak her mind. In many ways she was an inspiring role model, especially when compared to most other women of her generation.

Yet I also had an opposing set of feelings, which I could only express through my fears. As I neared adolescence, I was horrified at the prospect of my body changing and my impending development into a woman. It was the early 1960s—women wore beehive hairdos and emulated the perfect wife as modeled in the TV show *Father Knows Best*. I could see that as people grew up, men's lives expanded while women's lives contracted. Men went out in the world and followed their ambitions; women became innocuous helpmates who cooked, cleaned, mothered, and managed the daily routine. It felt to me like a death sentence—like being a huge jack-in-the-box about to be mashed into a little metal can—and I wanted no part of it.

I also dreaded growing up because of my father's rage and violence. Many girls, including me, whose formative years took place in small-town America in the 1950s, absorbed the cultural message that their ultimate happiness lay in marriage. Getting a good man was the prize as well as the quintessential measure of one's worth. I struggled to reconcile this vision of "happily ever after" with my raging father as my template for men. Longing daily for escape from his tyranny, the last thing on earth I wanted was to end up chained to another man.

So I spent several years singing the *Peter Pan* song "I Won't Grow Up" and begging my body not to develop. I wore pants and tailored shirts, refused my mother's offers to teach me to cook, and sought refuge in nature and solitude. The only thing I ever did with a Barbie doll was to build it a car.

Of course, my body had its own plans. "Now you're a woman," a Kotex pamphlet proclaimed, as if that were some kind of honor. Throughout my teen years I suffered from severe menstrual cramps, which I sensed were an expression of the rage I felt toward my body for betraying my wish to live free and true to myself. Years later, my cramps ceased after I discovered in therapy that I wasn't actually angry to be female—just angry to be pressured to conform to society's dictates for females. Over time I learned to stay true to my vision for my life regardless of society's propaganda about women as helpmates, sex kittens, and baby makers. I clawed my way to the clear knowledge that I get to be myself and pursue my dreams, and to hell with everyone else's expectations.

But as a young girl, I only knew that the world grew smaller and more limiting for women, which I must have learned from my mother, my primary female role model. Since then, I've learned that *her* mother, though strong, always believed in the rightness of "respecting her husband," which meant letting him be the boss and have the final word. Dora was a strong woman, up to a point, and so was my mother. I suspect Dora paid a price for giving up her power, although I don't know the details. But my mother certainly did, and her inability to stand up to my father compromised her vision of raising her children in a nurturing, supportive environment.

Paradoxically, she took out her frustrations on my sister Kathie, the younger daughter from my father's first marriage, who was a spirited, rebellious child and also a deeply troubled one from having lost her biological mother at such a young age. Kathie and I have enjoyed a close relationship as adults, and many times we've discussed family history and dynamics. Kathie remembers an incident when she was eleven and the family was eating dinner at a picnic table outside of our Fostoria house. When Kathie tried to cut corn off the cob using a table knife, the knife and corn went flying. Our mother started shrieking, chased Kathie inside the house, and hit her repeatedly. Kathie also remembers our mother frequently slapping her across the face if she showed the least hint of anger or resentment.

Our mother has described her own terrible temper as a child and being called a *vilde chaya*—a wild animal—by her mother. (This information, as well as her treatment of Kathie, supports my suspicion that her childhood was not as rosy as she remembers.) By the time she reached adolescence, she'd tamed that wildness, concealing it behind a nice-girl persona. I suspect that Kathie represented to our mother her own uncensored wildness, a part of her she needed to suppress in order to stay in her marriage, keep the family together, and hold her frustrations in check. In hitting Kathie, I believe she was beating down that rebellious voice within, the voice that kept saying her situation was unacceptable and had to change. As an adult, Kathie has developed compassion for the frustrations in our mother's life during that time, yet she also sees clearly that compassion doesn't excuse the behavior.

In the 1980s, our mother helped to found Homesafe, a domestic violence shelter in Ashtabula, Ohio. She spent countless hours supporting women to leave abusive partners and championing the right of children to grow up in a supportive, loving setting. Perhaps that work was her way of doing penance for not having protected her own children from abuse. Perhaps, too, it's easier to take a strong stand against abuse with less at risk personally. A therapist I worked with during the late 1990s once remarked that my mother could have stopped *all* the abuse in my family—perpetrated by both my father and her—by leaving and taking Mark, Rowan, and me with her.

I was close with my mother during many of my adult years. A shift toward greater closeness began in earnest one mid-1980s winter day in the kitchen of my parents' valley home in Ashtabula. We had a silly habit of calling each other Tiborg and Aalborg, after Aalborg Akvavit, an anise-flavored liqueur she was fond of. In a Scandinavian accent, I commented, "Aalborg, these winter days remind me of our childhood in Copenhagen, when we would spend afternoons skating on a frozen pond." She replied, "Tiborg, we can skate here just as well!" Then she started "skating"— sliding in a circle in slippered feet on the brick-red asphalt tile floor with her hands clasped behind her. I joined in, skating glee-fully with her for several minutes. This playfulness between us wasn't new, but what came next was a complete surprise. As I reached the side of the kitchen that opened to a utility room, she suddenly pushed me through the doorway, slid the door shut with a wicked sneer, and cackled, "Now the pond is mine, all mine."

I was shocked to see my mother behave that way, even in play. While I was growing up, she'd always presented herself as gener-ous and compassionate, disdaining even a hint of malicious in-tent. As an adult, I thought my mother lived a whitewashed life because she was so invested in being seen as altruistic, loving, and principled. In addition, she always played the part of the prude, with my father shielding her from swear words and risqué jokes. As I believe everyone has a dark side, her whitewashed persona seemed inauthentic and was an obstacle to my ability to trust her. When I saw her express her malicious, selfish side, even as a joke, she became more genuine to me. That event heralded the start of a deeper relationship between us.

In the years that followed, we shared our feelings, concerns, and dreams. We vacationed together, once at a cabin by a waterfall in Watkins Glen, New York, and several times at a lovely cottage on a private beach north of Mendocino, California, where we walked for miles collecting shells and reveling in the wild magic of the Pacific Ocean. We brought art supplies and drew wildflowers and seascapes, and we talked for hours at a time about goals, politics, nature, and family dynamics. Time and again we butted heads over a central conflict: her commitment to political and social ac-tivism versus my commitment to personal growth. She criticized me for being self-centered; I criticized her for ignoring the importance of inner work. But somehow we stayed connected.

Those years of friendship served as a foundation for our closeness around the time of my father's death and for several years afterward. I remain grateful that she and I were able to create a united front during his illness and that I was able to stand by her, and him, with loyalty. I'm also grateful to have had a period of time with my mother when her habitual defenses were relatively absent and her authentic self was much more available than usual. The fact that I had such an opportunity with both of my parents during that time made it all the more precious and poignant.

But in the years following my father's death, my relationship with my mother deteriorated, eventually to the point of estrangement. She underwent changes over several years after he died, and our rift was in part a function of those changes. Soon after his death, she asked me to let her know if she was changing. As I saw her become less present and more controlling, I shared my perceptions and suggested that she consider talking with a counselor. Each time I shared what I noticed, she dismissed me. At some point, I realized that although she'd asked for my input, she wasn't open to it and I needed to let it go. Reflecting on the truth that "you can't change anyone but yourself," I adjusted my behavior and expectations to the new reality.

My emotions during that time ran the gamut. I spent three months so angry at my mother that I felt as though I was on fire. At times I also bounced back and forth between feeling hardened against her and feeling locked into believing I should accommodate and keep peace at any cost. As I stayed with the process and allowed all my emotions to surface, I felt adrift and motherless for a while as I grappled with the break in our connection. My therapist at the time encouraged me to sit with the truth of my experience and fully grieve what I'd lost.

My work in therapy during that time was leading me to examine my psychological inheritance from my mother. As I unraveled that relationship and continued to work to heal the effects of my father's abuse, I discovered deeper layers of the internal chasm separating my compliant and angry sides. My compliant side was shaped by enforced silence in the face of my father's abuse as well as my mother's put-on-a-happy-face denial of family problems. My angry side was shaped by the assaults on my body and spirit and, as an adult, by my sure knowledge that child abuse is profoundly damaging. Over the years, I felt an increasing need to distance myself from my mother to continue to heal that internal chasm and create more choices than just the two extremes.

The gap between us grew wider as I became less accommodating in my quest for healthy middle ground. The more centered I became, the more I experienced my mother as covertly critical. The more I grew into the person I wanted to be, the less she seemed to like me. If I shared a story about speaking up for myself, she'd mutter under her breath, "Willful child!" When I let her know that I was uncomfortable with her comment, she denied it and proclaimed that she was "cheering me on" in living an empowered life. The discrepancy between how she treated me and how she claimed to feel grew to a point where, after quite a few attempts, it became clear that I could no longer have a straightforward conversation with her to address concerns. It felt as though we were swimming in an increasingly dirty fish tank and I was being asked to pretend nothing was amiss.

I was fine with letting go of the past and viewing my mother's behavior during my childhood through a compassionate lens, but I wasn't willing to put up with poor treatment in the present (from her or anyone else) or pretend I didn't notice the current gulf between her stated values and her behavior. The toll it took on me to participate in that dynamic was too great. A vast amount of my distress during my younger years was a result of growing up in a home where speaking out against injustice was encouraged but where I was silenced with regard to my siblings' and my own abuse; where following my dreams was championed but where I was regularly advised by my mother to settle when it came to a life partner; and where I was told I could be any kind of woman I wanted while being relentlessly prodded to be more feminine and compliant. When I was young, trusting my own perceptions and preserving my sense of self in the face of those contradictory messages was a monumental task. I wasn't about to endure that kind of treatment again. I had no idea how to have an authentic relationship with my mother, and I was unwilling to have an inauthentic one.

After many concerted attempts to resolve issues with her over the years after my father died, I realized that I needed to make peace with the futility of the situation. In 2007, I made the difficult decision to disconnect from my mother. The issues that directly led to the estrangement were serious and escalating, involving breaches of trust and my mother not taking responsibility for what she'd done. Although we no longer communicate, I still wish her well, and for reasons of both privacy and focus I choose not to share the details of our estrangement.

I wish I could have a relationship with my mother, but I can't. What went wrong was beyond my ability to change—much as I would like to think that self-examination would lead to that kind of wisdom. I miss the closeness she and I had, especially around the time of my father's death, when we shared so deeply and openly with each other. I still care about my mother, and I want her to be happy, to be surrounded by close family and friends. But I care about myself as well, and I have limits. Whatever she needed from me in the years since my father's death, I simply didn't have it in me to give. That understanding freed me from being locked in the "good daughter" role, dutifully attending to her needs at my own expense. Engaging in that dynamic was exquisitely painful and also harmful to my mental health. Cutting off contact with her brought me back into present time, no longer lost in an idealized future, wishing she were different so we could have a healthy adult relationship. I let go of needing her to change so I could be happy—no longer held her responsible for any part of my well-being or my fulfillment in life. Facing the reality of our relationship, consciously choosing my path in the face of that reality, and grieving what I'd lost helped me mature and eventually meet other losses with greater compassion, clarity, and equanimity.

Part II

TURBULENT TIMES

CHAPTER 6

Before the Crisis

My next-to-last visit to my parents' home before my father's illness and death happened at Thanksgiving in 1987, when I was living in Ithaca, New York. Thanksgiving was my favorite holiday, the one I made a special effort to spend with my family regardless of where I lived or the distance I had to travel. Despite the conflicts, I drew nourishment from our connection and shared values. Rich Jewish food and humor flowed freely, as did stimulating political debate. I treasured the tranquility and ever-changing nature of the Ashtabula valley, and I delighted in the company of Arran, my parents' bearlike golden retriever, and Nina, their feisty basset hound whose independence inspired us all.

My parents' dining room was too small to comfortably hold all of us for the Thanksgiving meal when in-laws, "outlaws" (unmarried partners of family members), and grandchildren were present, so we set up tables in the living room. That Thanksgiving, following a family tradition, we each shared something we were grateful for immediately after the meal. Suddenly my father barked, "I want this goddamn mess cleaned up—NOW!"

We froze. Dad was angry again. Once that happened, there was no turning back—or so we believed. My heart flailed in my chest, as it had all my life when terrorized by him. I squinted hard to see through the fog of family patterns to make out a hint of a new way to respond. Shaking, I took a deep breath, and out of my mouth came the words, "Have you ever considered that you can just *ask* for what you want? That you don't have to get angry—that maybe we'd cooperate just because we love you?"

My father fell silent. Self-consciousness replaced rage. After a moment, like an actor who'd just been handed a revised script, he said, "This mess is really bothering me. I'd appreciate if everyone would chip in and get things back in order."

We stumbled over a response, no more certain how to interact than he. Finally I said, "Sure—we'd be happy to."

My father took leave of us, heading for the bathroom. Perhaps his patriarchal habits caused him to think he was exempt from cleanup. Just as likely, he simply didn't know how to be with us without his anger, familiar as a gun on a cowboy.

No Thanksgiving tables were ever cleaned up faster than ours that year. In fast-forward we whisked plates, glasses, and silverware to the dishwasher, leftovers and salad dressings to the refrigerator, the navy-and-white Guatemalan tablecloths and napkins to the hamper. Pots were scrubbed in record time. The card table was rushed to the garage, folding chairs lined up in the front closet, the dining room table returned to its regular location. A speedy hand sweep of the floor, and our work was finished.

We lined up on the couch, breathless from our aerobic cleanup, suppressing giggles so Dad wouldn't hear. Emerging lighthearted from the bathroom, he looked around, thanked us, and asked if it was time for pumpkin pie.

I was never again afraid of my father. Although I didn't recognize it at the time, I had broken free of the psychological bondage I carried from childhood. The next time I saw him—my last visit while he was healthy—was by no means free of conflict, but I was free of my old pattern of being paralyzed by his rage and allowing its avoidance to run my life.

That last visit took place in 1990, the summer before his illness and death. I was thirty-eight and living in San Francisco.

I had flown back to Cleveland for two weeks to visit my family and spend time with Donna, a close friend in Detroit. By that time my parents had moved from their valley home in Ashtabula to a small two-story house in Richmond Heights, a northeast suburb of Cleveland. The house sat on an acre of land that backed up to a ravine and stream, offering my parents a much-needed connection with nature.

They had moved the year before at my father's urging. He wanted to live closer to Cleveland to have easier access to museums, libraries, and restaurants, and to attend Cleveland Orchestra concerts without a long ride home late at night. As well, negotiating icy country hills in winter taxed him, and the upkeep of the Ashtabula home had become a burden. He routinely mowed the meadow and the area around the house and cleared snow from the quarter-mile driveway. Maintaining a supply of firewood, although enjoyable, was exhausting work that required pulling fallen trees from the woods, sectioning them with a chain saw, splitting the logs with the Ellsworths' hydraulic splitter, and stacking the pieces. At seventy-two, my father was ready for an easier life.

My mother, reluctant to leave her beloved valley, had resisted the move for several years despite the culture and close friends that Cleveland offered. In hindsight, she suspected that my father might have been preparing to die and that moving back to Cleveland was part of that agenda. Years ago, she shared a story about Chuck and Milly, the friends with whom my parents had bought the land in Ashtabula. In 1987, when Chuck was seriously ill with cancer, he and Milly wintered in Florida. During the long drive back to Ohio in the spring, Chuck became gravely ill but didn't die until they reached their daughter's house in Athens, Ohio. My mother suspects that a similar concern for her well-being—her safety and access to emotional support—factored into my father's urgency to return to Cleveland.

The new home proved to be an adjustment for them both. My father felt constricted by the low ceilings and small rooms as well as by the lack of privacy compared with the valley. My mother missed greeting the river each morning and immersing herself in the peace of the natural world. Still, they adapted. "You make a decision, and then you make it work" was my father's modus operandi. The accessibility of Cleveland's classical music scene helped balance the sacrifices.

Music was an integral part of my father's life. For many years he played violin in the Ashtabula Community Orchestra. He and my mother frequently attended classical concerts throughout their marriage. He masterminded benefit performances for the Cleveland Orchestra and for Homesafe, the domestic violence shelter that my mother helped to found. He treasured an extensive collection of biographies of famous musicians and composers, many autographed, which he reread regularly and shared with family and friends. He also owned an impressive videotape collection of public television concerts. He derived great joy from watching a conductor or soloist labor over a difficult passage or feel the emotion of a poignant movement. Classical music enriched his life and sustained his spirit.

He transmitted his love of music to his children. We attended orchestra and chamber music concerts regularly as a family. Every winter we observed the Cleveland Institute of Music's master classes, a weeklong program during which famous musicians, including Josef Gingold, Mischa Schneider, and the Guarneri Quartet, taught gifted students. I loved the music itself, and I particularly cherished sitting next to my father as he watched a musician play with feeling. He soared with every fervent facial expression and stroke of a bow. I knew my father's passionate side by witnessing his great love of music and musicians.

My father first heard Russian violin virtuoso David Oistrakh when our family lived in Fostoria. He was wild about Oistrakh, and that concert began his long "love affair." My father rarely missed a nearby concert and read everything he could about the violinist. After shaking hands with Oistrakh at a Toronto Symphony Orchestra concert, he joked for days that he wouldn't wash his hand.

When Oistrakh died in 1974, my father corresponded with one of his biographers, a Japanese writer who lived on the West Coast. In a letter to the biographer, he wrote, "I miss him." My father's passion for Oistrakh's music created in him an almost personal tie with the violinist.

Oistrakh's grave is in Novodevichy Cemetery in Moscow, where many other famous Russians, including Chekhov and Prokofiev, are also buried. The cemetery is one of Moscow's top tourist attractions, but in 1989, when my parents traveled to Moscow, it wasn't open to the public. My father finagled a visit to Oistrakh's grave by convincing a tour guide to lie to the cemetery gatekeeper that my father was one of Oistrakh's American relations. My mother remembered the two of them passing Nikita Khrushchev's monument and then arriving at Oistrakh's—a tall pillar surmounted by a beautiful sculpture of his face and violin. In my mother's words, my father "embraced it tenderly and then just stood in silence, somewhere else in mind, almost like hearing the chords of the violin. It was a personal experience for him."

An even more personal experience was my father's relationship with Hyman Schandler. Hyman immigrated to the United States from Latvia in 1900 at age three. He began studying the violin at age nine at Bailey's Music School, which later became the Cleveland Music School Settlement. He started teaching there at eighteen and continued to teach for more than seventy years, as well as being principal second violin with the Cleveland Orchestra for thirty-five years. He also founded the Cleveland Women's

Orchestra in 1935 because (quoting from his obituary), ". . . he was concerned that many talented women musicians had no outlet for their musical skills in an age when women were still virtually excluded from the ranks of professional orchestras." The orchestra, still in existence, is the oldest women's orchestra in the United States.

My father began studying the violin with Hyman at age six. Over time as my father matured, his relationship with the warmhearted, compassionate musician developed into a lasting friendship. In later years, my parents would often visit Hyman and his wife, Rebecca, enjoying dinner and wonderful conversation. One evening, my mother once shared, when Hyman, no more than five three, reached up to bid farewell to my very tall father, he said, "If I had had a son, I would have wanted him to be like you."

My father responded, "If I could have chosen a father, I would have wanted him to be like you."

One morning during my 1990 visit with my parents, I awoke late on September 4 and came downstairs to make a cup of tea. My parents, finished with breakfast, sat in the den drinking coffee, reading the newspaper, and chatting casually. All of a sudden my father said, "Oh my" and grew silent and teary-eyed. My mother and I gathered around him and looked at the newspaper he was reading, only to see Hyman Schandler's obituary at the top of the page. Hyman had died at age ninety of congestive heart failure after several years of frailty and declining health. My father, profoundly saddened, delivered a moving eulogy at Hyman's funeral.

~

During that period of time, my work in therapy was helping me feel less a victim and more an active agent in my life. The previous Thanksgiving visit with my parents, when I broke my habit of freezing in the face of my father's anger, had been significant.

Since then, I'd thought about the code of silence in my family about my father's violence. I'd discussed it in recent years with my sister Rowan and my mother, but never with my father. This visit was the time.

My father and I were sitting in the den. I told him I was working on some childhood issues in therapy and needed to ask him something. He tensed. Nervous but determined, I asked, "Why were you violent toward us kids when we were growing up?"

A look of shame washed over his face. After a few moments, he muttered, "I don't know."

"Was it because of how your father treated you?" I asked.

"I think so," he replied.

I didn't need anything more from him; I didn't need him to apologize or ask for forgiveness or discuss the repercussions of his violence. All I needed was to speak the words aloud to him—to break the taboo—and have him not deny or defend.

When I visited my parents, I always wanted long hours with my mother and felt annoyed by my father's intrusions and his resentment of my closeness with her. While I loved my father and enjoyed him for short periods of time, living with him for more than a few days was difficult. He wanted everyone to play by his rules and didn't accept that others had different styles. He usually treated me like a disobedient youngster who needed continual reminders to behave and act responsibly. He hounded me to clean up my "shit" in the absence of any mess and monitored my every move to ensure that nothing in his home was disrupted.

One winter evening while my parents still lived in Ashtabula, I left pieces of an orange peel in a neat pile by the kitchen sink while I went to put on my slippers so I could take the peels to the trash barrel in the garage. When I returned to the kitchen, the peels were strewn across the floor. I asked my father what was going on, and he replied, "If you're going to treat my home like a dump, I guess I will, too."

His micromanagement set up a perennial conflict between us. After twenty years on my own, I was unwilling to play the role of a subservient, acquiescent child and resented his expectation that I would, so the visits were tense and strained. I always struggled to find a balance between sufficient time with my mother and a brief enough stay to minimize conflict with my father.

This last visit in Cleveland was no different. The tension mounted steadily in the final days; I felt no freedom to move without him telling me to lower my voice, do a chore, or get him something. If I tried to read a book in the same room with him, he demanded my constant attention, often as a child would—by tapping his fingers or making nonsensical sounds to interrupt my concentration. I was annoyed and eager to leave in order to be free of his intrusive energy and the battles that were always just around the corner.

We had a blowup the morning of my departure. I was trying to have a conversation with my mother at the breakfast table. He didn't want to hear it, so he said *dosta* ("enough").

I snapped, "Could you *please* let me finish my sentence before you interrupt?"

He snapped back, "Lower your voice—it's early, and I don't want the neighbors to hear."

I perceived his order as a control tactic; the nearest neighbors were seventy feet away, and I wasn't yelling. I stomped out of the room with an irritated growl.

When he and my mother drove me to the airport, he refused to hug or kiss me or say goodbye. I was furious that he carried his anger so far and frustrated that clear communication with him was so elusive. I was unwilling to placate him at my own expense and never saw much room to move in working out our differences—it was his way or not at all.

We avoided contact in the following months. My mother called when my father was out or sleeping, and I called rarely and hoped that my mother would answer the phone. After two months with no communication, I wrote him a letter, dated September 20, 1990, hoping to find a way to bridge the gap between us.

Dear Dad,

Since my visit, I've been thinking about writing to you and needed some time to clarify what I want to say. I wish our visit hadn't ended on a tense note, but sometimes it takes tension or confrontation to clarify the issues.

I'm uncomfortable being with you sometimes because it seems to me as if you need to have everything your way. It's very aggravating being told to hush every time I open my mouth. I get angry because I wish you'd let me be and not try to control things all the time.

I'm also angry with how you give orders. I find it rude that you tell me what to do rather than asking as if it's a favor I have choice about. It's a matter of courtesy and respect for me as your equal rather than as a subordinate you can order around. One way in particular that this shows up is when I'm doing something in the kitchen; you come in with your own agenda, and instead of saying, "Excuse me," you just say, "Look out." I'd like you to have the courtesy to realize that your needs aren't always first priority and that you might just have to wait a minute. And at the very least, saying "Excuse me" is called for.

I know that in the past I've catered to you in many ways because I've wanted to keep peace and avoid your anger. Often it's seemed as though we have to play your way or else you're going to take your toys and go home—that is, you shut down and wait for someone else to make peace. I'd like you to be more willing to meet me in the middle rather than require that I initiate a reconciliation by apologizing or meeting you completely on your terms.

I was angry that you couldn't at least be human toward me at the airport—that you couldn't bring forth a little caring despite your hurt feelings. I don't want to dance around your hurt feelings anymore or treat you like a little boy who needs to be protected. You're an adult who is responsible for your own feelings—responsible for how you choose to react in a situation—and I'm not going to tailor my responses and behavior to keeping the peace with you. My commitment is to be true to myself, to communicate honestly, and to bring forth as much love as possible. My commitment is not to doing whatever will keep you from getting angry or hurt. Getting angry or hurt are choices you make, and when you do, you can make other choices to remedy the situation. My hope is that you'll make choices that open doors instead of closing them, but that, too, is your choice.

I also want to clarify that I'm not interested in doing things out of guilt. We get in a tangle from time to time because you think I should visit someone. I don't think I owe Aunt Rose [his sister] *anything; if I go see her, it's out of my affection for her, and my decision will also take into account my other needs and wants. I'm tired of being called selfish because I'm operating out of my agenda instead of yours. From your vantage point it may look selfish, and you certainly have a right to your opinion. But I've done a lot of work in therapy to learn to live more true to my own values and experience, and to let go of the heaviness of what everyone else thinks I should do. So my preference is that if you want me to do something, you say, "This is important to me" rather than trying to guilt-trip me—and that you remember that I have free choice and won't operate out of obligation.*

I don't like the pattern of tension between us that only gets addressed later in letters. Because I have a long history of doing whatever it takes to avoid your anger and violence, I often don't think clearly when we have a confrontation—I only have an automatic response of wanting to get away from you—so I don't always know how to deal with the issues right when they're happening. Addressing some of this stuff in a letter makes space for me to be clearer and more authentic with you in person in the future. The old patterns need to be broken—because they're not working anymore—and this is hopefully a step in that direction.

My hope is that we can both remember to access the love we feel for each other even as we're shedding old skins and growing new ones.

Love, Kira

I felt strong in writing that letter—in naming and challenging old patterns of catering to his anger. I was proud of myself for dealing with him not as a subservient child but rather as an equal, and for refusing to allow him to pull rank anymore. I hoped by some miracle that he would hear what I was saying, but his response assured me that he hadn't.

Dear Kira,

Since your letter I have been doing some thinking, for I needed some time to clarify what I wanted to say to you.

I also wish your visit had not ended on a tense note, but I have to point out that I feel you cannot hang all the responsibility on my back.

First, let me point out that living in a smaller house with lower ceilings, my ears are more sensitive to loud sounds, and very often I ask Mother to talk softer and she understands what is going on. Perhaps I should have explained that to you when you came.

Second, let me point out that our blowup came about 7 a.m. with the windows in the family room wide open, at a time when our neighbors might still be sleeping. I try to have things quieter till it is later, or else close the windows.

But for the moment let's put aside whether I am right or wrong. I understand that you want me to speak gentler to you and not open my mouth like you did to me. You have a right to criticize me and suggest anything you want, but if you think that opening up to me like you did will make me more caring at the airport, you have to rethink what happened.

Your letter makes a good case with a long list of complaints to which I must say that I could come up with a long list, too, but I choose not to do so.

To be honest, I don't really care who you visit when you are in Cleveland, and I shall try to remember not to suggest that you visit anyone.

I shall try harder to say "please" and "thank you," etc., etc., because you seem to need it. I don't.

But I also think that the next time we are together, I shall enumerate some of the things you do that bug the shit out of me.

Pops

I reviewed my earlier letter and saw that I'd written it from the perspective of my personal needs but lacking a tone that might build a bridge between us. So I tried again from a different angle (letter dated October 8, 1990).

Dear Dad,

Thanks for your letter. I'm not sure you took my letter in the spirit it was intended, and I want to clarify some things. My letter wasn't meant to blame you or to say that it's all your fault. It was meant to address some things that, for me, stand in the way of good communication between us. I was talking mostly about a pattern I see in myself—one that has grown out of family patterns (not only between you and me, but in the family as a whole)—that doesn't serve my mental health. I wasn't saying it's all your fault.

At the same time, for me it's important to acknowledge that some of the patterns originated in the atmosphere in which I grew up. It has had a significant impact on my life that I grew up in constant fear of your anger and violence, rather than feeling that you were my protector—someone to help teach me and make the world safe for me. (That's not to say you didn't teach me a lot or protect me in some ways—only that the emotional climate for me was one of fear.) That has shaped me in many ways, and much of the work I'm doing on myself these days is to heal from that.

I don't share these things with you to try to make you feel shitty about yourself. Although on one level it might look like that, I'm asking you to look beyond that. It's important for me to be able to look squarely at my life—to look at the forces that have shaped me and the assumptions I made about the world based on them—rather than to tuck away pieces of reality because looking at them is too painful or because it's breaking a family taboo. That part of it I do for myself, for my own healing.

I'm sharing this with you because I've come too far to live in fear anymore, and you've been the most important person I've lived in fear of. It keeps me stunted and paralyzed to live that way, and I can't do it anymore. So when you get angry, it's my challenge to not just run away or cry or try to placate you, which is what I did as a kid—but rather to stay centered and at the same time try to keep the channels of communication open between us. It's not easy for me to do, but I know that's where my healing can come from.

I'm also sharing all this with you because I'd like for you to be able to step into my shoes for a minute and feel some empathy for me. I'm not saying you have to, but it's something I'd like. Again, this isn't about blaming you—it's about asking you to let yourself feel things from my perspective for a moment.

One of the things that happened many years ago that allowed me to feel closer to you and more committed to our relationship was when I began to realize what you went through while I was growing up—the meat-packing plant burning down and your health stuff and the stress of being the provider and all that. Understanding that stuff allowed me to quit seeing the whole situation just from the perspective of my needs and helped me empathize with what you went through and some of the pressures that influenced your behavior. And, of course, knowing a little about how your father and brothers treated you also helped me better understand you and the forces that shaped you.

What I'm asking is for you to see a little of my life from that perspective—what's made me who I am and what I need to do to heal. It doesn't necessarily mean you feel guilty and rotten and blame yourself. Maybe it simply means you accept the part you played and be compassionate with yourself and acknowledge that you did the best you could at the time. And maybe it also means using the greater wisdom and love you now have to continue working to break the old cycles.

Most of the time I don't blame you for what happened. Yes, there's a scared little girl inside who still hurts from those times, and sometimes she's angry—but mostly sad that she never felt safe with her dad and never had the closeness she longed for.

But mainly I think about how this pattern has been passed down from generation to generation from way, way back. You got some of this from your dad, who acted this way out of his pain—and he got it, I'm guessing, from his dad or parents, and so on. I don't care anymore whose "fault" it is—I only care that it stops. And I don't even know that my way is the way to stop it, but it's the only way I know how to: by talking, by acknowledging the monsters that hide in the closets, by speaking the truth, and by keeping my heart open.

I always think you see me as the enemy when I bring up hard stuff between us—that for you, the trust is gone and we're back to square one. I'd like to ask you to instead entertain the possibility that we might be on the same team and that we're not starting over each time we have something challenging to deal with.

That's why I couldn't understand why you were so cold at the airport. I'd like not to feel that your love is conditional and that I have to earn it (by "behaving," or whatever). I think there's a way we might relate to each other as though we just know we're on the same team no matter what comes up that needs working through.

Love, Kira

I wrote that letter less than three months before my father got sick, and my mother found it in one of his favorite books after he died. I still wonder how he received it and how he would have responded if we'd had more time.

Sometimes it feels tragic that our last interactions before his illness and death were such struggles. I would have preferred to look back on some smooth sailing. But I also know that the conflicts were born of my deep conviction that I needed to break old patterns in my relationship with him—to step fully into adulthood as well as to stop repeating destructive patterns of mistrust and defensiveness in intimate relationships. I was thirty-eight and had never had a relationship that lasted longer than a year. I was with Dominic, my first love, for nine months when I was twenty-six—my only foray up to that point into the realm of authentic relationship. When Dominic ended things, I was so devastated that I retreated into my shell, more certain than ever that being vulnerable was a bad idea. That retreat reinforced my childhood conviction that relating to others was best accomplished through invisibility, self-protection, and couched hostility.

Refusing to cower in fear or be kept in line by my father's anger was an important step, one I had dreamed of taking for years but only once before, at the Thanksgiving gathering, had the nerve to carry out. I wish he and I could have had more time to explore the new direction I proposed in my second letter—learning to be allies—but perhaps there was nowhere to go. Perhaps he never would have understood, and maybe the only thing to do was what I did: to state unequivocally that I wasn't going to live by the old rules anymore.

Our next exchange occurred when he was first hospitalized for cardiac fibrillation, two weeks before he contracted the staph infection. He was in stable condition when we spoke on the phone. All the conflict between us was washed away—I only cared about his well-being. I sent him love and joked that the nurses had better take good care of him or they'd have to answer to me.

I spoke with him one last time before he began to lose mental clarity. He was back in the hospital because medication wasn't properly regulating the arrhythmia. Our conversation is forever inscribed in my memory. I had been working in therapy with Paul on my relationship with my father. Two days before the phone call, in a particularly significant session, I tapped into an intense anger I had never felt before, a dark energy that completely disregarded the well-being of others and sought to annihilate everything in its path. I wanted to take time during the session just to be with that energy—to feel it and get to know it. But Paul rushed me through the emotional experience into a cognitive understanding of the rage, determined that I accept the energy as part of me. I resented him for prematurely pushing me past my feelings.

I was to become profoundly grateful to Paul for trusting the impulse to push me. When I spoke with my father on the phone two days later, he wasn't in an especially attentive mood, but I forged ahead anyway, feeling an inchoate urgency to tell him about that therapy session. I told him about the energy I had met in myself—a dark, raging energy I had always attributed to him that I now realized lived in me as well.

"You mean I'm not the bad guy anymore?" he asked.

"No, Dad, you're not the bad guy anymore."

Perhaps the moment was too raw for both of us since we ended the call quickly amid awkwardness and embarrassment on both our parts. But I had said it, and he had heard it. And in all the horrors that followed, nothing could erase that interchange between us.

CHAPTER 7

The Infection Rages

The evening my father's staph infection turned critical—also the first day of the Persian Gulf War—my brother called me in San Francisco. Mark's voice broke as he said, "Daddy's real sick." I knew my world was about to change forever. I flew to Cleveland the next day, and my sister Kathie picked me up at the airport. Together we headed for the hospital.

Since I'd had almost no previous experience with serious illness and had only once been in an intensive care unit, I didn't know what to expect—I only knew I wanted to see my father and be with my family. As Kathie and I entered our father's room, he began to weep. I was startled to see him so vulnerable in my presence; I'd never seen him cry except during *Lassie* episodes and when I was five and he told me his mother had died.

I realized that only a serious illness would make him drop his normal defenses, yet I also considered it a breakthrough that he could show his vulnerable feelings to his children, regardless of the cause. During the next week I saw him cry several more times—on another occasion when he saw me, upon hearing his two-year-old granddaughter's voice on the telephone, and while talking with close friends in Florida about his great fatigue and need of a vacation.

When I saw him weep as I entered his room, I became concerned that my presence might be troubling to him. My sisters and brother lived in Ohio, and I suspected that my cross-country trip indicated to him the gravity of his condition. Assuming his tears were anxiety about his health, I reassured him that I made the trip because I loved him and wanted to be with him, which only made him cry more.

My father's thinking during that time wavered between slightly and severely confused. My siblings and I kept asking if he knew what had happened and kept repeating the facts to him: he had an infection, the infection was causing confusion and physical weakness, the doctors knew what was wrong and were treating it, and he was going to get better. He cried and said, "I hope so."

My mother later told me that my father was crying because he was allowing himself to feel his family's love, as well as because he realized he meant enough to me to be worth my long trip from California. His illness blasted through his defenses and allowed him to feel how much I cared about him. It also blasted through the walls that had kept my heart hardened against him. It wasn't until I faced the possibility of losing him that I realized how deeply I loved him.

~

My presence quickly turned into more than a visit. My mother and brother had been on twelve-hour shifts by my father's side for days, and both were exhausted by the time I arrived. Although I had arranged to be in Cleveland for ten days, I hadn't anticipated stepping into the role of a primary caretaker, yet it soon became clear that I was needed in that capacity. My sisters were unavailable—Rowan was dealing with health concerns and a recent car accident, Deedee was preparing to move out of state, and Kathie held a job and attended college three hours away in Columbus. I began the vigil at my father's side.

My mother had arranged for my father to stay in a room with a couch, a table, several chairs, and plenty of space for visitors. She or I, or occasionally Mark, stayed with him around the clock.

The doctors explained to us that my father was experiencing "sundowner's effect," being relatively coherent and functional during the daytime but losing many of his mental faculties at night. He was often quite unmanageable after dark—even more cantankerous, obstinate, and willful than usual. Although ill-equipped to get out of bed by himself due to trembling and a compromised sense of balance, he would suddenly try to stand up, all two hundred pounds of him—a formidable challenge to try to catch if he were to fall. He was also disoriented, often heading off in the wrong direction to find the bathroom and responding belligerently if anyone tried to turn him around. My mother generally stayed overnight since she felt best equipped to care for him during that difficult time.

I arrived early each morning to sit with my mother and hear about the night's events, my father's condition, and her state of mind. Then she left to get some sleep, and I stayed with my father until late afternoon, when Mark took over. I had expected to keep my father company and help with whatever he needed—getting him a drink of water, reading to him, calling a nurse if needed. What I hadn't bargained for was hospital politics. At times it seemed as though the system was distinctly designed to keep my father from being treated well.

The doctors who cared for my father were, almost without exception, top-notch experts in their fields who were also deeply in touch with their humanity. At no time did they treat either my father or any family member with less than complete respect. Many other hospital personnel, however, were exasperating. The nursing staff was not equipped to provide around-the-clock attention, yet as family members we often had to fight for the right to stay with my father in situations that clearly called for constant companionship. In addition, several authoritarian-style nurses felt that my father might grow too dependent on our help and maintained that, for his own sake, he should develop the initiative to care more for himself.

My father was in no shape to grapple with self-care. Perhaps the nursing staff didn't realize he was so seriously ill or emotionally fragile. Perhaps they didn't know how headstrong he was, how determined to do exactly what he wanted, whether or not it was in his best interests. Occasionally when he tried to get out of bed, he'd ask me to help him up, which I wasn't strong enough to do. If I buzzed for a nurse, he would furiously blurt out that he didn't need anyone else's assistance. I realized that his real rage was about feeling helpless after being so independent and capable all his life. It was counterproductive as well as disrespectful to treat him like a disobedient little boy who should have known better than to get out of bed. I learned to handle those times by stating my own needs: "Dad, I'm not strong enough to support you well, and I'm worried that I'll hurt my back if I try. I want to call a nurse so neither of us gets hurt." He always responded positively to that. He demanded not to be robbed of his dignity even in the midst of relative helplessness. I cherished his fierceness and finally heard the message he'd been expressing all his life: "I refuse to be treated with less than full respect."

Another frustrating protocol was meal selection. Each afternoon, a dietitian asked my father to fill out menu preferences for the following day. I helped him select foods and then returned the menu to the dietitian, whereupon she erased three-quarters of his choices and told me that he couldn't have a certain thing because his liquids were limited or something else because he was on a renal diet. Infuriated, I asked her to cross off the foods he couldn't have *before* giving him the menu, but she ignored my request. Each day was a variation on the same scene.

He went from regular food to kosher and back again, hoping to find something at least minimally palatable, with no success.

During this time, one of his favorite nurses came in at lunchtime while he was struggling to eat something completely tasteless. "How's the food?" she asked. Without skipping a beat, he turned to her and growled, "Garbage!"

Card from Mark:

> Front: *Here are five words that just cannot*
> *be said often enough about hospital food.*
>
> Inside: *It tastes like buffalo shit.*
> *Get well soon!*

My father finally refused to eat any hospital food, so we smuggled in frozen yogurt from the cafeteria several times a day. At one point, authorized by his doctor, we brought him Chinese carry-out. It was the only time in the hospital when I saw him look forward to eating. He asked for a dish called Happy Family. It brought tears to my eyes to think that all he wanted was to be with his "happy family."

Finally the doctors, realizing that my father was hardly eating at all, became concerned enough to suspend all dietary restrictions just to get some nutrients in his system. My mother went on a shopping spree—shrimp, sharp cheddar cheese, stone-ground crackers, peeled grapefruit sections, and a Hershey's chocolate bar. It was to be his last meal, and I'm glad it was food he loved.

~

My mother often slept little on night shift, yet she waited around much of the following day to talk with doctors about my father's condition. After many days on this schedule, she became severely exhausted and needed a night off to catch up on sleep. No one was available to take her place overnight. I asked the nurses whether he would be adequately cared for without a family member present and was assured that all would be well. I made certain they knew how to reach us in case we were needed, and I made a point of telling two nurses as well as the social worker that under no circumstances was my father to be put in restraints—that they should call us to come if he became unmanageable in any way.

That evening several siblings and I were unwinding at Mark's house when the phone rang at 11:45 p.m. It was my father. "I just called to say hello and see what you're all doing," he said. Several of us talked with him, told him we loved him, and said we'd see him in the morning.

When I arrived at 8:00 a.m., my father was in a seriously disturbed state, withdrawn and uncommunicative. I kept asking him what was wrong but got no response other than a hurt, furious comment about hating the hospital and wanting to leave. I knew he was experiencing a setback, but I didn't understand the cause. When Mark arrived at 5:00 p.m., it became clear what had happened: Dad had been put in restraints the night before. Mark found them on the floor behind the bed. When he asked what had happened, our father got an angry, shamed look on his face and said they'd treated him horribly and told him to quit acting like a baby.

My mother exploded to the head of nursing that it was unacceptable that restraints had been used despite our clear instructions to the contrary. My mother also pointed out that her role at the hospital was to care for her husband, not to keep incompetent staff in line. She made it clear that the nurses involved were not to interact with my father again. Sure enough, when the night nurses came on duty, one of them was among those who'd been assigned to my father the night before. My mother and Mark had her removed from his care in a matter of seconds.

～

As disturbing as many aspects of the hospital time before my father's surgery were, those days were also inspiring and revelatory in many ways. I thought of the effects of his illness partly in psychological terms—that the infection had exposed a vulnerable layer underneath his character defenses. This type of opening happens slowly and gently in successful psychotherapy, within the protection and safety of a good therapeutic relationship and the therapist's solid understanding of the process taking place. The therapist can provide the client with a framework for working through emotions, thoughts, and behavioral changes that surface.

When circumstances break through deep defenses in a non-therapeutic environment, the outcome is much less controlled because no one functions in the role of the psychotherapist, tracking the changes and providing the client with a frame of reference. Situations of this sort can be terrifying to someone who doesn't understand that the changes are in the service of healing and who only knows that the old ways aren't working anymore. A fear of losing one's sanity may arise.

I viewed many of my father's emotional changes through this lens—that the illness had broken through his normal defenses, exposing much of the raw, vulnerable layer underneath. I knew he needed safety around him since a terrifying lack of safety during his childhood had no doubt created the defenses in the first place. I sensed that the compassion, love, and uncritical support of his family were more important than ever before. I became angry whenever anyone approached him with a parental, disciplinarian stance, whether saying he should shut up and eat his food or warning that he shouldn't become too reliant on our care.

I clearly saw the danger in viewing everyone through the same lens. I imagine that nurses see many patients who give up the will to live, becoming psychological invalids who rely on others to care for them. It follows that nurses would work to counteract this tendency, but they need to recognize that this approach does not apply to all patients. For my father, letting another person help him was a great breakthrough—to acknowledge that he wasn't an island apart, that he did have needs, and, most importantly, that he trusted us to stand by him with loving care. This emotional healing was a crucial aspect of his condition, and I was committed to seeing that he got the support he needed. Just as my mother functioned as his advocate to ensure that his physical needs were met, I was drawing on my psychological training to ensure that his emotional needs were met. I felt grateful that I had done enough work on my relationship with my father to understand some of the forces operating in him, and that I could step outside of our historical conflicts and honor his needs.

My mother and I talked many times about his "softening"— the miraculous change taking place that allowed him to be vulnerable with us, opening his heart and accepting that he was loved and lovable. We recognized it as a great healing in itself, yet we also hoped he would recover and have the opportunity to live with us in that softer state. She and I spoke of how we imagined the family would be with him less defensive. We both knew of the many patterns in our family system held in place by his defenses and the ways we had adapted to them. We longed for time with him with an easing of those patterns.

As I watched my father soften, I seemed to be witnessing the melting of his day-to-day ego-invested personality and the revelation of a shining layer of essential self. I found myself called upon to accept the changes in him and the new person he was becoming. If I clung to an old notion of my father who had to behave consistent with the past to fulfill my needs or expectations, I would be denied access to the radiant soul he was revealing himself to be and the profound healings available during this time. Conversely, releasing my old notions of him and letting him become someone new unveiled a tender man I loved deeply as well as a mystical level of reality far different from our habitual ways of interacting.

Because my father withdrew physical nurturance when I entered puberty, I grew up craving closeness with him, which I experienced as an almost physical ache. It was a longing to be hugged and to feel trusted, cared about, cared for. That longing was healed during his illness.

One day at the hospital, I was alone with him for a twelve-hour stretch. He was exhausted and restless at the same time, and I kept asking how I could help him be comfortable. Finally, he said, "Let me lie down on the couch with my head in your lap." I was astounded that he would allow me to be with him in such a close way. After feeling shunned by him for decades, I finally felt valued as someone who could offer him support and tenderness. The nurse on duty wouldn't allow him to lie on the couch for fear that he'd fall off, so I sat crosswise at one end of the bed, and he slept for two hours with his head in my lap. Time stopped for me—I was with my father, and we were being peaceful together.

On a different day, as I sat next to him on the bed holding his hand, he tilted his head over until it gently touched mine. He was saying, in his own language, that he knew I was right there with him. Years of distance and pain dissolved in that moment.

We also had fun times together. Because my father loved classical music, a portable cassette player and many of his favorite tapes stayed in his hospital room. One afternoon when Rowan and I were visiting, he sat in bed conducting to the music with a blissful, faraway look on his face. Talking with Mark on the phone, I commented that Dad was conducting with both his hands and his toes. Mark jokingly suggested I ask why he wasn't also conducting with his testicles. When I relayed the question, Rowan remarked that he was, but that we couldn't see because of the bed sheets.

Another time, as a Brahms violin concerto played by David Oistrakh came to an end, I playfully bowed as though I had been the soloist. My father gave me his classic "What kind of wiseass behavior was that?" look and proceeded to flip me the bird. I loved him fiercely in that moment—loved that he held onto his humor and fire, even in his incapacitated state.

~

During one of the days I spent with my father, he rested in bed while I sat on the couch reading *Shoeless Joe*, a meditative, mystical novel that was the basis of the movie *Field of Dreams*. In the midst of a relatively peaceful afternoon, my father suddenly stiffened and grimaced in great pain. I immediately called a nurse. Within fifteen minutes, the room was abuzz with all the specialists who had been caring for him during the previous week. Soon after, he was whisked away for a barrage of tests. When the results came back, Dr. Vlad Vekstein, the supervising cardiologist, called a family meeting.

Tests revealed that the staph infection had settled and was festering on one of my father's heart valves. Since the infection had already burrowed into heart muscle, it was fortunate that the situation was discovered before it killed him. However, he needed to undergo valve replacement surgery right away.

The prospect of open heart surgery was quite a shock to us, as we'd hoped the staph infection could be treated successfully through less invasive means. We'd all been on an emotional roller coaster during the previous week, thinking one moment that the infection might be under control and the next moment receiving a distressing report. We were so emotionally depleted from the ups and downs that we didn't quite trust any news, good or bad. But the thought of Dad undergoing such a serious procedure was deeply troubling. We clung to each other for comfort, grateful that Dr. Vekstein, who had become close to our family, described the situation and options in compassionate and straightforward terms. Surgery was scheduled for the following morning to stop the infection before it could do further damage.

The next morning, I was sitting with my father and holding his hand when the anesthesiologist came in. After a series of routine questions, he paused and then said to my father, "You look upset. Are you upset about something?"

My father was silent. As the anesthesiologist left the room, I rushed after him and demanded, "Why in the world would you ask that question? He's about to have open heart surgery. Do you think he might have something to be upset about?"

Soon after, the surgeon, Dr. Mark Botham—a serious, spare, quietly compassionate man in his thirties—came into my father's room to explain the procedure. He told my father, "This is about one percent up to me and ninety-nine percent up to you. Are you going to go for it?"

My father said, "You're damn right, I am." We were buoyed and comforted by his fighting spirit.

In retrospect, I believe my father's words were said for our benefit—that he knew on some level he wasn't going to survive but wanted us to think he went out fighting. Earlier in the week during an unusually revealing meeting with a social worker, she asked him whether it was "his time." At first he replied that he didn't know, but later in the conversation he said he had taught his family many things, and now he was going to teach us how to die with dignity.

At 8:00 a.m., family members gathered to kiss my father and wish him well during surgery. We understood the gravity of his condition as well as the risks of the surgical procedure he was about to undergo. Many of us had tears in our eyes as we shared our good wishes, aware that we might never again talk with him. My mother accompanied him, holding his hand as he was wheeled down the hall to the operating room.

During surgery, we waited together—talking, crying, meditating, praying, telling jokes, playing cards. Light moods were subsumed by fear so intense that none of us could stay present to it for long without feeling crazy. We supported each other through the lengthy surgery and reminisced about our father's many wonderful qualities.

During the day, I wrote the following in my journal:

> *Many times I've wrestled with the question* How could this happen? *and spent sleepless nights agonizing about how a trivial bit of carelessness* [the ambulance driver-medic being ungloved] *could cause my father this severe illness and life-threatening surgery, as well as the terrible toll on the family.*
>
> *Today, while waiting for my dad to be taken to surgery, I found some peace. I began to think of his medical condition symbolically as well as literally. I imagined the infection in his heart and envisioned the valve as a place where metaphorical toxins collected in his body—all the pain he's lived with for more than seventy years that has caused him to shut down and has limited his ability to give and receive love. Through this illness, he has undergone an amazing process of breaking through blocks to feeling—letting in how much we love him and crying without restraint. As he moves into this new way of being, the obstructions are collecting at one site so they can be removed.*

Seeing his illness through this new lens was powerful. My focus shifted from *Why is this happening to us?* to *What are the lessons and deeper meanings?* This new perspective brought a modicum of comfort and serenity amid the turmoil as well as a yearning to lift the veil that had kept this deeper vantage point separate from everyday reality.

I knew, however, not to use this perspective as a substitute for feeling the painful emotions of fear, grief, and anger. Experience had taught me that ignoring those feelings would drive them deep inside, where they would fester and ooze out in unconscious, destructive ways. However, this other reality could be experienced alongside the pain. As I opened to this new perspective, I marveled at the insights it accorded. I was also baffled as I thought about the difficult ways we humans grasp life lessons. Why do I have to lose someone to acknowledge how much I treasure him? Why do I need such traumatic events to learn not to be ashamed of my tears?

Opening to the lessons during my father's illness and death attuned me more finely to that other reality. I began to invite the awareness so that it wouldn't need to manifest as a two-by-four knocking me over the head. I hoped to learn to sense it as a gentle wind brushing my cheek, a whisper in a quiet moment urging me to open.

Chapter 8

Coma

At 11:00 p.m., a nurse notified us that my father had come through surgery and had been moved to the recovery room. We were allowed in to see him two or three at a time. My mother and I went first. We'd been warned that his face would be puffy and swollen, and that he'd be attached to tubes and monitors. Somehow I didn't see any of that. In fact, my experience wasn't a matter of seeing at all, but rather a sensing—an awareness of energy. I was awestruck in my father's presence as I absorbed the truth of who he was, how *big* he was. I realized the great courage he possessed in enduring this illness and surgery as well as throughout his life. With the veil of his personality lifted, I was perceiving his essential self.

My mother, Rowan, Mark, and my father's sister, Rose, had similar experiences in the recovery room. Perhaps the essence we encountered was his soul in the process of leaving his body. Or perhaps we, too, were stripped to our essential selves and more able to perceive with soul-level senses.

The doctors explained that a state of deep unconsciousness is common following life-threatening surgery. They predicted that my father would probably be comatose for several days, possibly a week. Family members took this news, as well as the reality of his coma, lightly because we understood his condition to be a normal stage in the healing process. We were advised to visit him often and to talk to him since hearing familiar voices might bring him back to consciousness. During most visiting hours of every day, at least one family member, often more, sat at his side, reporting the news of the day, telling him we missed him, asking him to wake up.

I was troubled that many of the medical staff, who only knew my father in this state of unconsciousness, had no sense of him as a person; they only saw a body attached to machines. Because I believe so strongly in the power of thoughts, I suspected that the more they could conceive of my father as vital and healthy, the more positive their energy toward him would be. My mother and I took to the hospital a beautiful photograph of my father holding Sasha, their golden retriever puppy—an image of almost portrait quality that conveyed my father's dignity and power as well as his gentleness. That picture remained on the bulletin board in his room for the duration of his hospital stay as a reminder to us and the medical staff of his wholeness.

～

I returned to San Francisco a few days after my father's surgery. I felt a strong pull to be with my family, yet I was also concerned about other commitments, primarily my master's program in counseling psychology. I needed to finish one minicourse and put other courses on hold.

Each day in San Francisco, I checked in with myself about when to return to Cleveland and came up with fuzzy ambivalence. *If the answer isn't clear*, I realized, *it's not yet time to make the decision.* That insight helped me sit more comfortably with the uncertainty; I trusted that I'd know when it was time to go. One morning I awoke certain it was the day to fly back to be with my family. I also sensed a need to be unpressured by time restrictions, so I tied up loose ends enough to be gone for several months.

Paul, my therapist, supported my decision. He said that because the experience of my father's critical illness would always be with me, it was important to make decisions that wouldn't leave me with regrets. His advice helped clarify that my priority was to be with my family, and it also guided my decisions while with them. Remembering to conduct myself in a way I could live with later kept me in touch with my gentleness when circumstances invited anger and confrontation. It helped me be aware of my right to set boundaries and the importance of honoring my needs and limits. And it connected me with a sense of inner balance I had been cultivating in therapy.

As I returned to Cleveland to once again immerse myself in the crisis, my efforts to stay centered paid off. Looking back on that time, I feel free of regret. Of course I've had questions, and times when I looked at my behavior like the tail of a sea creature mostly obscured by water and asked, "What was *that*?" I got glimpses of parts of me I hadn't known were there, parts I later worked to understand and integrate. But no remorse—I feel at peace with my conduct.

～

As I sat with my father, I often made strings of small rainbow-colored origami cranes as symbolic prayers for peace and healing—a meditative way to put my hopes for his recovery into concrete form. I also talked with him, held his hand for long stretches of time, and meditated to connect with his energy.

I decided to try a technique I'd learned years before called *active imagination*, developed by noted Swiss psychiatrist Carl Jung. Active imagination is a way of exploring material in the unconscious through creative fantasy. Art, dance, music, writing, and other activities can be considered active imagination in that they harness the power of imagination to actively engage with the unconscious. However, I use the phrase more narrowly here to refer to calming the mind and engaging in an active daydream or internal movie with the intent to explore an issue. The stage can be set by asking a question or requesting a person to appear in one's mind and then simply staying open to the flow of imagery that unfolds. Setting the stage can also be accomplished by "reentering" a dream scene where it left off and using the imagination to explore where the action might lead next. Active imagination can facilitate insight and allow access to deeper aspects of the self.

After quieting myself at my father's side, I asked for an image to come to me about his illness and coma. I saw him sitting at a picnic table in the Ashtabula valley in a spot where no table actually exists, beyond the far end of the old red building we used on weekends before the new home was built. In the image, I was sitting next to him and saw him put his arm around me and hold me, as I'd longed for him to do so many times. Then he said he had things to tell me. In my mind, I asked him to wait and allow me to soak up the good feeling of being close to him. He held me awhile longer, and then I moved back so we could talk.

He said he loved us. I saw him hugging several of my siblings and then my mother with an embrace that showed how deeply he loved her. I knew by watching the two of them that he also felt her love for him. In that moment, they looked like true soulmates, as though they had released the power struggles that often characterized their day-to-day relationship. Then I asked him what was happening—why he was in a coma and whether he was going to come back to us. I saw him flying in another space, far away, and indicating that he thought he was already too far from us to return.

Later that day, as I took in the surreal truth of his comatose state and all the medical equipment, I grappled with the tormenting question of his health crisis being an accident. Before the illness and surgery, my father seemed to me to be a vital man still in full possession of his faculties and zest for life. I couldn't grasp how this could be his time to die or how a medic's carelessness could set in motion the events leading to his death. I searched for a perspective that would bring me some peace.

The next morning I awoke with a new awareness about my question—a knowing that had come to me overnight. I remembered that for several years my father had been talking casually about death, commenting that he was getting old and wouldn't be around much longer or joking that something or other was going to kill him. Every time he spoke like that, a family member would berate him for it. "Don't talk that way—you'll make it come true," I'd warn. Or someone else would say, "Of course you'll be around then," chiding him for "giving in" to getting old.

That morning, I realized he had been trying to tell us that his time was nearing. He was thinking about dying and wanted to talk about it, wanted support—but we wouldn't listen. We gave him the clear message that it wasn't acceptable to leave or to talk about death with us. Death meant failure, losing, giving in—the sorts of things our father would *never* do.

Regardless of whether his death was truly an accident or whether it was simply his time to go, I began to understand that death isn't a failure at all—just the next adventure. My father deserved to die without risking the loss of our respect. I vowed to listen more openly in the future and to honor people's sense of right timing about their death.

This understanding served me well many years later when my friend Susan's mother died. Martha had lost her husband the year before and was deeply grieving his death. Then, after unsuccessful hip replacement surgery and a drug-resistant staph infection, her doctor told her she would never walk again. Facing the prospect of life in a wheelchair and an inability to care for herself, she chose instead to end treatment for the infection and stop nutrition. Although she was given up to three months to live, she died the day after making that decision with her four daughters at her side, all of them certain she had willed her death. I respected Martha's right to choose when to die—no decision is more personal—as well as her daughters' courage in allowing her to choose freely.

During my father's coma when I began to consider that it was his time, I felt prompted to discuss with my family his right to let go and die. I thought back to an experience many years earlier in a dentist's office when a dental hygienist canceled an appointment with me that she rescheduled for the following week. When I arrived, she told me that her father had been injured in an accident and was comatose. She spoke of her family's long hours in his hospital room, telling him his work wasn't yet done. Her story evoked my heartfelt empathy as well as a strong sense that it would be more appropriate to *ask* whether his work was done than to *tell* him it wasn't.

I also recalled a letter I'd received from my father a few years earlier. He'd written to all of his children to let us know that he had been experiencing some heart-related symptoms. His doctor had recommended an invasive diagnostic test that my father had refused. I suspect it was at that point that he came to grips with his preference to die with dignity rather than undergo traumatic procedures or live in an enfeebled state.

As I sat with my father in the hospital, I felt it important that my family support his right to let go—so important, in fact, that at first I forgot that we also had a right to state what *we* wanted. So it took time before I could say to him, "If it's your time, I support you," and also "I have a strong preference in the matter. I want more time with you. I want to celebrate this softening and enjoy unconditional love with you."

At my father's bedside, I talked about the possibility of our family living day to day with conscious love in our lives. Years earlier, in preparation for spending an afternoon with a woman who was ill with cancer, I meditated to see if I could sense an emotional or psychological component of her illness. It came to me—and she confirmed it as true—that she longed to live peacefully and didn't think it was possible to do so in the earthly realm, so she felt drawn toward death in hopes of finding that peace. Similarly, I had the sense that my father didn't know it was possible to live in the earthly realm and have relationships on the level of conscious, unconditional love. I wanted him to know that kind of love could exist in the real world, not just in fantasy. Consequently, many times I spoke to him about the opportunity to wake up and experience love and closeness with his family.

~

Most visits with my father were peaceful. I basked in his presence, savoring the energy in the room and the heartspace I shared with him. I was there to give him love and to let him know I supported him.

However, as the weeks passed with no lightening of his coma, I began to face the possibility that he might not wake up at all. For two days I was flooded with grief as I felt the full weight of the prospect of losing him. I craved physical contact, trying frantically to soak up those last days before he might be gone forever. I wept as I massaged his feet, stroked his hands and arms, rested my hand on his heart.

At some point it became clear that the emptiness I was feeling—the void I was trying to fill—was not that of his imminent death but rather his absence during my life: the loss I carried from the lack of ongoing support and closeness with my father. A craving for physical contact had been with me since childhood, as had the sense of never getting enough of his tenderness and love.

Once I identified the source of the emptiness, I returned to a sense of peace, no longer trying desperately to fill the void before it was too late. Realizing I was never going to completely mend the pain of my childhood gave me space to grieve my father's impending death, which felt distinct from mourning our difficult relationship and its toll on me, a task I could work on over time. That realization also gave me space to soak up the loving contact that was available in the moment. His critical illness opened the full force of my need for him, and I discovered the healing balm right there—contact with my father that was loving and peaceful.

A few days later I told him that I felt free with him for the first time in my life. Unable to build walls or distance himself from me, he could only lie there and accept my presence. I shared my exhilaration about finally bringing my authentic self to our relationship. I began to think about the things I wanted him to know about me, things I'd always kept private because I thought he wasn't interested, wouldn't understand, or would tease or ridicule me. He was now a captive audience, and I also imagined that perhaps he was now in a place where he could hear what I wanted to share and was able to relate to me at a soul level instead of from the limitations of his personality. Whether truth or metaphor, it brought relief and helped me speak openly to him.

Dad, it was awful growing up in fear of you. I wanted to be your little girl, safe in the comfort and protection of your love, but I felt terrorized by you. You didn't honor my sensitive feelings or treat me with kindness. Instead, you intimidated, teased, shamed, and silenced me with your rage and violence. I've spent twenty years working to heal from the effects of that, and it's been a daunting journey. But I've finally reached a point where I'm no longer willing to live in fear.

I'm learning to be present with myself—to stay with my feelings instead of shutting down when I get scared. And I'm learning to help others stay open when circumstances threaten their aliveness. I'm going to find a way to help people live healthier, more whole lives. And I'm going to do that myself, as well—to be the creative, passionate, idealistic person I was born to be. No more hiding out from myself or the world.

I told him those things, even though I imagined that in his current state he already knew. After all, this was more for me than for him. Once and for all, I stood in the presence of my father and spoke the truth of my life—my feelings, values, beliefs, and dreams.

I also used the technique of active imagination to create an opportunity for my father to speak. Again, whether real or metaphor, it felt important to create a window for an exchange rather than a one-sided communication. Since no one really knows what happens when a person nears death, I was inclined to be open to all possibilities and to treat my comatose father as I would have treated him if he were awake—as someone deserving a turn to speak.

My inclination was shaped by an experience six months earlier. Emmett, a family friend, was comatose and dying of cancer. Fran, his wife, had been agonizing over her unfinished communications with him. I shared with her my belief that a person in a coma receives on some level what is spoken, and I suggested she tell him what she needed to say to feel closure. So she spent time talking with him, telling him what she needed him to know. As I meditated the night before Emmett's death, the question came to me, "What does *he* need?" I imagined sitting by his side and asking him, and internally I heard him say he wanted the opportunity to tell his wife some things as well. My sense of this was so strong that I called Fran and suggested that she sit with him and let him know she was there to listen.

Similarly, one day when I visited my father in the hospital, I felt prompted to use active imagination to give him an opportunity to communicate if he had anything to say. I drew the curtains and asked the nurses to leave us alone. I breathed deeply for several moments to center myself and reach a meditative state, then sent my father the thought that I was there to listen to him. I told him if he had anything to say, he could imagine sending it with great intention and it would reach me.

Whether real or imagined, what came to me brought comfort and relief. He asked why I was there. I told him I wanted to be with him because I loved him dearly and wanted him to feel the full measure of my support. In my mind, he kept asking similar questions—"Why do you keep coming here? What are you doing here?"—as though he had to work to grasp the depth of my commitment to him. Then he said, "I can't tell you how much your love is healing me."

Tears came to my eyes as I imagined him fully taking in the love I felt for him. I responded, "I can't tell you how much your love is healing me," as indeed it was. My father's illness burned away the antagonism between us, which had blocked my openheartedness. His softening created a sense of safety that allowed me, in turn, to soften and heal.

~

Because of my father's passion for classical music, we employed it as much as possible in his healing. We arranged for him to wear a Walkman and listen to tapes after his surgery. We were buoyed to see him in the recovery room wearing headphones, with one of his favorite pieces playing. It was gratifying to feel the support of hospital staff in respecting our wishes, as well as to know that they, too, included music as a possible resource for healing.

My father wore a Walkman during most of the coma. We brought a selection of his favorite tapes and replaced them each week. We urged his nurses to play the tapes as much as possible and to rotate them rather than simply turning the same one over and over. For the most part, they were extremely cooperative. When my mother entered his room, she gently removed the headphones and said, "It's intermission time, honey." Before leaving, she restarted the music, saying, "The concert is about to begin again."

We'll never know what he heard or on what level he heard it, but surrounding him with something that had brought him so much joy during his life could only have been beneficial. Ultimately it's not important whether his heart or his soul was humming along with the world's great musicians.

One day I read a newspaper article about a music therapist who worked with comatose people. The article quoted a former coma patient who said that music helped bring him back to consciousness by reminding him what was beautiful in the world and why he might want to return. As I read his words, I thought that if anything could bring back my father, it would be music.

With the permission of the intensive care staff, my mother and I asked Ed Ormond, a violist with the Cleveland Orchestra and a close family friend, to serenade my father. Two hours later, the room was filled with Ed's music—first Bach and Vivaldi classics, then Yiddish folksongs. Mimi, Ed's wife, leaned over my father and tenderly sang some of the words. The music continued for thirty minutes until, overcome with emotion, Ed had to stop. It was a magical time. Nurses and other caregivers in the unit stopped to listen. We were all entranced by the music, by the power of the prayer we were offering through Ed for my father's recovery. Even though it wasn't strong enough magic to wake him up, it was a rich gift, a final concert to sweeten his journey.

CHAPTER 9

Death

During the fifth week of my father's coma, in the absence of any improvement, his neurologist, Dr. Gerald Grossman, ordered a new round of tests. When the results were available, my mother, siblings, and I requested a meeting with all the doctors who were instrumental in my father's treatment and care. Dr. Grossman told us that the tests revealed considerable brain damage that was believed to have resulted from a portion of the staph infection migrating to my father's brain during surgery. Dr. Grossman assessed that my father would never recover a meaningful quality of life—that the brain damage was so extensive that even if he awoke, he would never be able to feed himself, move around on his own, or perhaps even understand speech. We all knew that he would never want to live under those circumstances. He and my mother had talked at length about that issue many years earlier, so she was clear about his wishes. As a family, we chose to execute his living will and discontinue life support. In the midst of the horror, it was comforting to feel united as a family; no one disagreed or fought the decision, and my mother didn't have to make it alone.

He was taken off life support on March 4. Visiting hours were extended so family members could stay with him all day and long into the evening. Unlike previous visits, we now usually came in groups, both to bolster each other and because we wanted as much time with him as possible.

Knowing he would soon be gone forever, I treasured my visits with him even more than those of the preceding weeks. These were my last moments to hold his hand, look at his beautiful face, feel the strength of his being. Even a coma couldn't diminish his presence and vitality. I soaked up his energy, knowing I'd lose that luxury in a few days.

I searched my soul for other things I wanted to share with him before he was gone—lingering thoughts about our relationship, my life, what he had given me. It seemed important to be as complete as possible, to not hold anything back.

My sister Rowan and I sang to him. We often sang him the chorus of "Tender Shepherd" (from *Peter Pan*). It became even easier to express my tenderness to him, something I'd rarely, if ever, been able to do while he was healthy. He'd been so adept at deflecting it with a joke or by pretending to be too busy. Now there were no obstructions, and all the love I felt for him came pouring out. It was a strange balm in the midst of the grief—feeling free to share affection I had always held inside.

During those last days, we thought and talked about my father's memorial service. We felt uncomfortable planning it while he was still alive, but since his death was inevitable, we wanted to plan a service that would be a fitting tribute. So we talked, wrote, made arrangements.

Two days after life support was removed, my father's appearance changed dramatically. His face became sunken from the lack of fluids. Death was imminent.

That night my mother stayed with him in his hospital room. I'd planned to meet her as usual early the next morning to sit with her for a while before she left to get some sleep. Just after 7:00 a.m., several minutes before I planned to leave the house, the phone rang. It was Mark calling to say that Dad had just died. Our mother had been at his side.

I rushed to the hospital and ran to his room, where I found my mother and Mark. I cried and cried, first as I hugged them, then as I hugged my father. It was a surreal time. I'd never been with a dead person before and had expected to be terrified, but I wasn't. It was just my father, at peace after a long battle, having endured so many violations to his body that I was relieved his suffering was finally over.

Soon after, the rest of the family arrived. We cried and hugged each other as well as our father. At one point we stood in a circle holding hands, including his, and felt ourselves a complete family for one last time. We stayed with him for more than an hour, talking about him, recounting some of his more outrageous escapades, alternately weeping and laughing. The nurses outside our closed curtain must have thought we were crazy, but we didn't care. Part of honoring Dad and our love for him was remembering his spunk, his wit, all the things about him that had brought us joy.

When it came time to go, we each said goodbye in our own way. He was getting cold; his chest and belly were still warm, but his hands, feet, and face were chilled and bluish. I didn't want to stay much longer. I hugged him and kissed his forehead, thanked him for all he had given me, wished him well on the next part of his journey, and said goodbye.

～

We stayed at the hospital briefly, partly to remain in our circle of comfort, not wanting to leave the security we derived from holding onto each other. We also wished to thank several doctors and nurses who had been exceptionally kind during the ordeal. We collected personal items—the cassette player and classical tapes, the beautiful photo of Dad, valentines we'd given him while he was comatose, origami birds that hung by his bed.

Amid sadness and bewilderment, I felt an underlying current of what I can only call "rightness"—not so much rightness that my father died, which was out of our hands, but a sense that we had done what, on a deep level, we were supposed to do: care for him well and consciously, wrap him in unconditional love during his last days, and send him on his way knowing how dear he was to us.

The next few days were a whirlwind of kind friends, meals cooked for us, and planning for the memorial service. My siblings and I each wanted to speak, as did several relatives and close family friends. We wrote eulogies and mapped out the details of the service—blue irises (my father's favorite flower), the Yugoslav rug we would take to the hall, the classical trio—Ed Ormond, Harvey Wolfe, and Judy Berman—who would play Mozart's *Divertimento in E-Flat Major*. We created a service that honored him fully.

Rowan and Mark made a tape of his favorite music to play before and after the service. We unearthed photographs that portrayed him in various arenas of his life—as a schoolboy, young man, husband and father, woodcutter, violinist, businessman, gardener, grandfather, dog lover—and created two collages to display at the back of the room where the service was to be held. One of the collages included some Bill Staines song lyrics (from "The Boats They Come, and the Boats They Go") that seemed to capture an aspect of my father's essence:

He just leaned into life as it went on by,
And like a sail on the wind, oh, it carried him high

I made and hung long strings of rainbow-colored origami cranes, larger versions of the ones I'd made during my father's hospital stay. One of those strings still hangs in my home.

The service was everything we wanted, a fitting tribute to this man we treasured so deeply. We clung to each other and wept openly. I felt completely at ease with my feelings with no shame or sense that I should hide them. I was moved to see that more than two hundred people had come to pay tribute to my father, from hospital nurses and doctors to a man who had worked for him twenty years earlier.

I wrote the following and read it at the service:

Some of you know that my relationship with my dad was not easy. My relationship with my mom has been much less difficult; she has always been the safe one for me, the one who wanted to share my inner world, the one who let me be her friend and support her. With my dad, it wasn't such smooth sailing. The love he and I felt for each other wasn't always apparent in our day-to-day interactions. And yet the struggles all got washed away with his illness. Before his surgery, I spent long days helping him and keeping him company in his hospital room. Those were some of the most precious times we ever spent together. I had nothing to work out with him, no place to get to. I was there to love him, pure and simple. And he loved me back just as purely and simply, and let me in, in ways I've always longed for—with his gentleness and affection, and by asking for help and trusting that I was there for him.

I feel blessed to know such unconditional love for my parents. And I wonder why people don't usually live day to day in the experience of unconditional love. Maybe if we did, we'd never go through the lessons we're here to learn with each other—we'd just love each other and then love some more. But even while we long for things to be smooth and easy, if we're lucky we treasure the growth that comes from the struggles.

From my dad I learned to stand up for what I believe in, to not be intimidated, to fight City Hall. I learned from him to follow my own path, to not live by other people's limitations, to be able to stand alone when necessary. I learned to accept in myself the dark energies I had always attributed to him—and in learning that, I became more whole.

I also learned many easy lessons from him—to laugh and be playful, to express myself with music, to dream big and trust that I have it within me to attain those dreams.

One of my dad's last lessons was about love—about opening his heart, letting in the love that was there for him, and accepting how deeply he was cherished. He learned that lesson well; his heart was healed at the end. And he left us the legacy of living with our hearts less obstructed and more open—of knowing more clearly that love is really what we're here for.

Some of what I learned from my dad came from following his example. Some came from freeing myself from his influence, and some from working on my own to break loose from constraints that bound him. But the way of learning doesn't matter; what matters is that the lessons got learned—we did with each other what we came here to do—we exchanged the gifts we had for each other.

There's a story of a Buddhist monastery whose spiritual leader died. Soon after, his successor was found weeping in his room by a disciple. "Why are you weeping, Master?" asked the disciple. "Death is merely an illusion. There is no such thing as separation. We are all one."

"Yes," said his master. "Death is an illusion. There is no real separation. But my eyes miss seeing my friend, and so they are crying."

I will miss my dad—I'll miss his energetic presence, his playfulness, his delicious smiles during a good concert, his childlike delight at seeing a baby hawk, his stories of travels around the world. And yet I know he will be with me—in my heart, in my memories, and also as a living presence I can always contact.

Safe journey, my friend, my teacher, my fellow adventurer… and thank you.

Several days after the memorial service, my immediate family gathered for a private ritual at the river by the valley home where my parents had lived for fifteen years. Again we had blue irises, one for each family member. One by one, we cast our flowers into the icy water, saying goodbye to the man who was our father, husband, grandpa. At dawn the next morning, restless and unable to sleep, I walked downstream and found several irises caught on the banks of the river or frozen in ice. I dug them out, walked out on flat rocks into the river, said goodbye again, and set them free.

Part III

CURRENTS OF HEALING

CHAPTER 10

Gentleness and Authenticity

I remained in Cleveland for a month, living with my mother and taking time to absorb the shock of my father's death. Those days were bittersweet. We spent long mornings drinking tea in the den and talking about the hospital time. We each found in the other a safe and willing partner with whom to share our feelings. Sometimes we fell apart with grief; at other times we basked in our mutual love and the strength of bonds forged during two months of supporting each other through the nightmare. We also spent time reading and cherishing sympathy cards that overflowed with love and respect for my father. Following are three of the most memorable ones.

Dear Bea,

We really do not need to say how much we loved Lou, his love of life and beauty, his loyalty to friends and family, his always ready helpful nature, and his great love for you, is Lou to us.

I don't know if you remember, when we had our last supper together in that restaurant, as we went out to our car, the last thing Lou said to us was, "Do you realize one of your lights [headlights] *went out?" How true! One of our lights truly went out, but in our memory Lou will always shine.*

Love you! Ed & Mimi (Ormond)

Dear Bea,

I didn't know Lou was ill, so I was all the more shocked when I read his obituary in this morning's Plain Dealer. *His death brings to mind all the pleasant hours we spend together out at your Dewey Road [Ashtabula] retreat . . . I was always much taken with his great warmhearted enthusiasms—for books, for music, for birds and flowers, for the land, for everything of human interest. In his passing, we have lost a man of great scope and great talents. I shall miss him and long remember him.*

With deepest sympathy, B.G.

Dear Bea,

I was saddened to hear of Lou's death and deeply affected by it. Some people leave their mark on me instantly. Lou was such a man. He impressed me as a highly complex individual who lived intensely, loved intensely, and believed in both himself and a basic sense of justice. Yet, he always was willing to seek and grow.

I was personally deeply touched that he came to see me [for counseling] *about a personal problem. He transcended generational stereotypes because he felt I could help. It spoke to his ability to break conventional molds.*

I read [a copy of] *the memorial service and found myself crying at several points. I was crying for the loss of a great man who touched so many.*

I want you to know that I found inspiration in realizing who he was and the message he left—live life to the fullest and never compromise your inner core.

I thank him, through you, and hope that each day gets a little easier.

With love, J.A.

We also received moving letters from two of my father's doctors:

Dear Bea,

Thanks so much for your lovely note. You were extremely generous in your compliments. I have grown very fond of you and your family, and being with you during those difficult weeks of Lou's illness did not feel like work for me. I was also touched and honored to be included in the close circle of family and friends following your husband's memorial service.

I was truly saddened by Lou's death. He was a truly remarkable man whose life had significant impact on everybody he came in contact with. It was the highlight of my days to spend time with him. In spite of his illness, he was always capable of an insightful comment or question that would elevate my spirits.

I have certainly enjoyed getting to know you and your children. You are all an example of unity and inner strength that is so essential in coping with life's surprises and pitfalls. I am sure that Lou would have been truly proud of all of you during those most difficult weeks following his surgery.

Hope that life is going on and that things are falling back into their routine. If you ever want to talk or if there is anything I can do, please do not hesitate to call. Please give my best to Deedee, Mark, Kira, Kathie, and Rowan. Take care of yourself and remember to get plenty of rest.

Sincerely yours,
Vlad (Vladimir) Vekstein, MD
Director, Coronary Care Unit,
The Mt. Sinai Heart Institute

Dear Mrs. Silverberg:
I would like to once again extend to you my deepest sympathies at the passing of your husband. Although I only knew him for a short time, he was a pleasant and caring man. The support that you and your family gave to him during this period of illness was second to none I have ever seen. It is comforting to see families so committed to the well-being of a loved one and to abide by his wishes in this period of medical demand. I will always remember your husband, as will all our medical staff and hospital staff, and the ease with which you made our delivery of medical care to him pleasant. Our thoughts are with you in this time of sorrow.

Sincerely, Mark J. Botham, MD
The Mt. Sinai Heart Institute

After a month in Cleveland, I returned to San Francisco for my final quarter of graduate studies. As I went through my daily routine, I kept noticing how poorly I handled anything that required effort. I quickly became drained when completing a reading assignment, talking with professors or other students, or doing even minor chores such as washing dishes. This change from my typical energetic self left me feeling out of sorts.

After a few weeks, I realized that this fatigue was a natural response to the stress and loss I had just experienced. I remembered that I needed time to heal and that the best prescription for recovery was to be patient and gentle with myself. In therapy, Paul told me it often takes people a year or more to get through the bulk of grieving. One day I caught myself thinking, "What a drag—I'll have to be nice to myself for a whole year." Then I laughed, noticing that I viewed self-nourishment as a burden. I realized that my father's illness and death were powerful training in being more loving with myself. I pledged to remember to do it not just for a year but for the rest of my life.

I became annoyed by suggestions from others to "bounce back" and "get on with my life," which countered my promise to be gentle with myself. Some of the messages came from acquaintances, such as fellow students, who encouraged me to be strong or keep busy; others came from people closer to me, including my housemates. I learned to simply state that I needed to take it easy and heal gently from my recent loss. Speaking up for myself strengthened my conviction that I had a right to grieve in my own way. It also afforded me an opportunity to teach others that there's another option besides the "buck up" mindset so prevalent in our culture.

This mindset creates the illusion that the only way to deal with loss is to bury it. Grieving people are often perceived as stuck because other people can't distinguish between stuckness and consciously attending to one's healing. If a person is in denial about the loss, or if, years later, his or her life is frozen in the moment of loss, the person is likely stuck and would benefit from counseling to help emotions to move more freely. However, if emotions are moving and the person is developing a different relationship with his or her grief over time, the process is probably working just fine. In this case, the best support a friend or family member can give is to convey faith in the process of working through the grief. Counseling can benefit these people as well; since welcoming intense emotions is generally shunned in our society, a grieving person might appreciate the extra support to delve freely into feelings and reflect on the insights they bring.

At one point my sister Kathie shared with me a conversation with her friend Ann (a therapist!) about our father's death. Ann asked how family members were handling the loss; Kathie said some were doing better than others. When Ann asked who was having a hard time, Kathie mentioned my name. Ann said she was surprised because I was so "spiritual." After all, I supposedly believed everything happened for a reason, so why couldn't I simply accept that my father's death was meant to be? Kathie echoed some of Ann's viewpoint and expressed concern about my palpable pain.

Hearing that, I grew even clearer about the importance of allowing feelings instead of blocking them. My goal was not to get *past* the feelings but rather to *allow* them and let them move through me. I wrote the following to Kathie:

> *How things look to you from the outside isn't necessarily how they are on the inside. I can well imagine that it looks as if I'm suffering or not "getting on with my life." But please hear this: the inner work I'm doing IS me getting on with my life. It's me making the most of this time, taking advantage of the opportunity to work with my issues at a deeper level. I've known for years that some inner poison was preventing me from living fully. Now something's happened that's metaphorically split me wide open. I finally have the opportunity to access the poison and clean myself out, and you bet I'm jumping at the chance to do that. I certainly wish Dad hadn't needed to die for me to access this stuff, but this is how it happened, and I'm going for it. From my perspective, this is me looking at the good that comes from this experience and, more than that, living it—letting it move through me and change me. I WANT to be changed by it. I don't want to carry around all that baggage anymore. And it's irrelevant to me that from the outside it might look as though I'm feeling funky a lot of the time. From my perspective, I'm learning to accept more of myself, to welcome my emotions, and to live more authentically.*

I learned a great deal about not apologizing for my emotions or minimizing them in the interest of being "appropriate." And I came to believe that the lack of mental health in our culture is directly related to suppressing feelings. Emotions are the psyche's

natural mechanism for healing; to suppress them is to deny ourselves the opportunity to clean out psychological debris and move
on. It's a common belief in our culture that when it comes to painful experiences, people can simply "give it up," but in reality this
is only achieved through the natural process of emotional release.
It's said that we replace all the cells in our bodies every seven years;
we can similarly refresh our psyches by welcoming our feelings,
working through them, and letting them help us shed distress as
well as beliefs and emotional habits that suffocate our vitality.

Several days before our father died, Rowan and I were walking down a hospital corridor after leaving the cafeteria. We had
been talking poignantly about losing our father and were full of
emotion, crying on our way back to his room. A group of nurses stopped us in the hall, and one of them, apparently trying to
offer comfort, asked, "What's wrong, girls? Dry your tears and
cheer up—you'll feel better." Her suggestion irked us. We'd both
worked long and hard to learn to welcome our feelings, and we
viewed our tears as healthy rather than as something to repair
or eliminate. We replied that we were having an appropriate response to a devastating situation. We felt good about not buying
into prevalent notions about being strong in the face of adversity.
In fact, the experience reconfirmed my belief that being strong
often means allowing vulnerable feelings to surface instead of
blocking them.

Three weeks after my father's death, my mother and I attended a memorial concert performed in my father's honor by the
Ashtabula Chamber Orchestra, in which he had played the violin. Before the concert began, an orchestra member who'd known
my father for many years came over to ask how we were doing.
Aware of the socially proper thing to say—"We're doing okay"—
I instead tearfully shared the truth: "We miss him a lot." She
became teary-eyed and said she missed him, too. I appreciated the

authentic exchange with her, so different from the empty niceties of social conventions.

During this time I became less focused on who I thought I should be for other people and more guided by a sense of being true to myself. One day in San Francisco following my father's death, I was upset before a therapy session and felt a need to yell and hit pillows to release some of the energy. I didn't think I could do that in Paul's presence. I realized how much of myself I hadn't shared with men—a direct consequence of growing up with my father. I'd learned early to seek safety by hiding and by toning myself down. I sensed that to bring more of my authentic self to therapy would be an important step. In fact, I didn't think I'd be ready for an intimate relationship until I could bring my intensity and a matter-of-fact "This is who I am" stance to my relationship with Paul. Therapy seemed to be my training ground. I tested out yelling in Paul's office and was relieved to discover that no bolt of lightning struck me down. Little by little, I learned to show him more of my authentic feelings.

As I explored this issue, I began to understand that I didn't want to live in my father's shadow anymore or be constrained by the limitations and imprinting of growing up under his rule. Even more than not *wanting* to, I was no longer *willing* to. I hadn't lived with my father for twenty years and had worked tirelessly to heal the past, yet I was still so tied to my programming from him. Paul told me he'd heard of many people only beginning to express themselves fully and do their real work in the world after a repressive parent died. Amid the grieving, a new "me" was being born. I was healing internal divisions—acknowledging the full range of my feelings instead of walling off the ones that countered my self-image or programming. I was feeling fiercer *and* more tender, loving *and* hating my father, missing him *and* feeling more free with him gone—and becoming much more whole in the process.

~

After my father's death, I felt a growing need to spend more time in Cleveland. The ordeal of his illness and death, as well as my return to San Francisco for three final months of graduate school, had exhausted me. I welcomed the opportunity to grieve with my family, work on my healing, and be temporarily relieved of the pressure of supporting myself.

I drove from San Francisco to Cleveland in early July of 1991. I'd originally planned to spend two months in Cleveland, but I stayed for four. My hope was to find a part-time job, so after a week of relaxing, I threw myself into the job search. I was baffled as I encountered one obstacle after another—few advertised jobs, awkward phone conversations, bungled interviews, miscommunications at every turn. Prior to attending graduate school, I'd worked for ten years as a graphic artist, always finding employment with ease. I expected the same in Cleveland but soon discovered that graphics positions were scarce. Still, I believed the right job would appear at the right time, and I grew increasingly miserable at my lack of success. During this time, I was in a foul mood most of the time, angry that life wasn't working as smoothly as I expected it should.

I finally registered with a temporary agency and went out on an assignment. Working as a receptionist for thirty people, I lasted five hours. I returned to the agency and requested a job with limited people contact and clear-cut responsibilities. I was placed in an ideal position—office assistant to a kind, gentle man who had previously worked alone. I lasted for one morning, quitting as soon as I learned I was required to use a parking garage. Seven weeks of using the hospital parking garage had left me panicked the instant I drove into one.

Amid tears and frustration, I admitted to myself that I wasn't emotionally equipped to be working. After overfunctioning during my father's illness and then losing him, I needed a reprieve from the challenges of being out in the world. I saw that I'd come to Cleveland not to get a job but rather to heal. And life, far from not working smoothly, was working just fine; I simply had missed important cues. It was as though life had been gently shaking me to release my grip on being employed. When I clung more tenaciously, it shook me harder to get my attention. Finally I surrendered and decided to use my stay in Cleveland to give myself what I really needed: time to mend and heal, time with family and friends, time to write.

As I made that choice, my world opened up again. No longer did a black cloud follow me around, sabotaging my efforts. I basked in the feeling of aligning with the wisdom of my authentic self, noticing how different it felt from trying to *make* something happen. I vowed to remember that and to recognize in the future when I was trying to force a situation that wasn't right.

I also felt the power of giving myself what I needed. Mainstream American culture supports the strategy of keeping busy and burying pain. The cost of this approach is apparent in the prevalence of poor mental and physical health and also in the fact that many people aren't happy with their lives. In choosing to nourish myself and address my pain instead of swallowing it, I felt like a revolutionary refusing to live by cultural norms. What would the world be like if we all gave ourselves the gift of choices that nurture us?

～

Months after my father's death, I was reading *The Seat of the Soul*, a book by Gary Zukav that includes a discussion about the power of thoughts. Zukav writes eloquently about our inner negativities being mirrored outwardly in such things as racism, sexism, and war. He expresses a belief that directing anger toward another person only causes harm in the world.

While I believe that anger, when wielded wisely and consciously, is a powerful tool for defining boundaries and can serve as a creative force in relationships, Zukav's words still caught my attention. I found myself thinking about my anger toward the ambulance company responsible for the staph infection that caused my father's death. Every time I drove by its headquarters or saw one of its vehicles around town, I was overcome with anger and sent its employees hateful thoughts. Before reading Zukav's book, my reaction felt natural, given my father's wrongful death sparked by the carelessness of medics.

After reading the book, I became intrigued with the thought that I was creating more negativity and unconsciousness in the world by sending out hate and anger. I also knew that harboring unresolved anger and resentment can compromise the immune system. "It's only human," many would say, as if to excuse it or cease to question it further. However understandable my anger was, I felt as though I was spreading poison when I sent out hateful thoughts. In a wondrous instant, I realized that I had another option. I could instead send the ambulance company healing thoughts in hopes that its employees would do their jobs with greater consciousness. I understood that no one intended to cause my father harm—the medics were simply careless in the moment, as we all are sometimes.

I began to look forward to driving by the ambulance company's headquarters as an opportunity to wish its employees well, and also as a challenge to expand my ability to love. I tried to be compassionate with myself when I saw an ambulance and could only bring forth anger, but those times diminished as I continued to work through my grief.

(Soon after my father died, my family filed a lawsuit against the ambulance company, claiming that his death had been caused by negligence on the part of the medics who administered an IV under unsterile conditions, which caused the staph infection. We sought legal recourse in hopes that the ambulance company, a private establishment, would be held legally responsible for the consequences of the medics' actions and that, by being subjected to legal scrutiny, would improve its standards of medical care. The ambulance company claimed immunity from liability based on an Ohio law that applies to public agencies as well as private agencies operating under contract or in joint agreement with a political subdivision—for example, 911 medics. After several years in the courts, a judicial ruling on November 13, 1995, denied the motion of the ambulance company for immunity, thus establishing the company's liability. My family felt satisfied that we had achieved our objective of legally establishing responsibility for the quality of medical care provided by private ambulance companies in Ohio.)

CHAPTER 11

Support During Grieving Times

My father's death was the first significant loss in my life. Because I lacked firsthand experience of how uncomfortable many people are with death, I was surprised at some of the reactions that family members and I encountered.

The day my father died, my mother and Kathie went to the mortuary to make arrangements for his cremation. The funeral director transacted business without offering even the simplest of kind words, such as "I'm sorry for your loss," and ended the meeting with "Have a nice day!" They were appalled.

I received meager support from my best friend during my father's illness. Donna and I had been close since college, with more than our share of friction but also a deep connection that had reunited us after an eight-year separation. Since reconciling, we'd traveled extensively together, attending personal growth workshops at the Findhorn Foundation, an intentional community in Scotland, and vacationing in Ireland, Hawaii, and the Southwest. Donna knew of my father's illness and my return to Cleveland. Living in Detroit, she could have easily visited for a weekend or at least called. As it was, I received two impersonal cards—the kind with chickadees on a tree branch and the words "Just Thinking of You" in gold script—but no personal message. I was shocked and saddened that she didn't offer any heart-to-heart support.

Caught in the daily demands of my father's illness, I wondered only sporadically, "Where is my best friend when I'm going through the hardest time of my life?" Distraught, I wrote her a brief note that included: "If you care about me at all, now is the time to show it." She called and angrily asked how I could question her regard for me, asserting that I placed unrealistic demands on her. As she continued, it became clear that the current situation was bringing unresolved issues between us to the surface. She thought I was too needy; I thought she was insensitive and self-absorbed. The crisis with my father tipped the scales so that we were no longer able to maintain our delicate equilibrium. Old conflicts, however, were irrelevant to my main focus—my father's illness—which, in itself, demanded far more emotional energy than I had. I asked Donna whether she could set aside her concerns for the moment and trust that we'd return to them when the crisis was over. She was unable to, so I chose to temporarily disconnect from her, irked that she couldn't respect the fact that I was in the middle of an emergency.

During the following year we corresponded from time to time. As we reviewed what had happened, she began to face her habitual pattern of denying the unpleasant things in life—death, pain, conflict, negative feelings. Raised to be a Pollyanna, she never learned to face adversity head-on. In addition, she'd been close with her grandparents since childhood and dreaded losing them, which heightened her fear of death. Although she and I wrote back and forth sharing pieces of our growth, I still felt her abandonment deeply and was angry that she couldn't acknowledge and apologize for the pain her lack of support caused me. (Much to my surprise, four years later, after a long silence, I finally received a heartfelt apology.)

Dealing with Donna's absence during my father's illness and death sparked much reflection on the topic of denial. Rationally, I understood her need to distance herself from death because it brought up terror and confronted her deep defenses. I couldn't fault her need to shrink from something so upsetting to her sense of emotional safety. Still, her denial and absence toppled the trust we'd shared up to that point.

I also realized that for years I, too, had been in denial—about her inability to offer emotional support. I saw that I'd been dependent on her friendship and had avoided raising concerns in order to minimize conflict. I needed to be hit squarely in the face with the issue of denial to realize the part it played in my own life and the ways it harmed rather than protected me. My hard lessons with Donna taught me to bring a fuller honesty to my friendships and to risk addressing problems, which I came to see as the only avenue for creating authentic, satisfying connection with others.

I began to ponder what it meant to "be there" for another person. I needed so much during and after my father's grueling ordeal. Dizzy with nightmarish images and feelings I had to release from my private inner world, I often wanted to talk nonstop about the pain—my father's, my mother's, my own. Liz, a good friend and no stranger to family loss, having sat with her mother before losing her to cancer, was an angel of the first degree. She never backed away from my pain, never let herself be scared by it; she listened and accepted with shining love.

My friend Janis also offered me substantial support. My buddy since fifth grade, she'd lost both parents and a brother under traumatic circumstances. Jimmy, her nineteen-year-old brother, was found dead in the bathtub after a sliver of bone from a leg fracture traveled to his heart. Janis's father died of a heart attack, followed by her mother's yearlong decline and eventual death from lung cancer, with Janis as primary caretaker. She knew firsthand about the challenging emotions that arise when a loved one dies.

Janis never backed away from my tears, even when they erupted without warning on a San Francisco bus or in a supermarket. She met me lovingly wherever I was, never asking for consistency.

She had no problem with me missing my father one minute and hating him the next. And because she knew my father and had spent time with him over the years, she was able to empathize with both extremes. She knew firsthand his funny, feisty side and also his volatile fury. Not only that, but she could pull stories out of her memory from twenty-five or thirty years earlier that affirmed my feelings. She had witnessed his dictatorial "End the discussion!" when a conversation made him uncomfortable, and she knew how quickly he could go from relaxed to rageful.

As the sympathy cards poured in at my mother's house, I read scores of comments about what a wonderful man my father was. I thought he was, too, but that definitely wasn't the whole story. (To my mother's credit, she didn't deify him either.) The adult daughter of a family friend wrote that my father was the gentlest man she had ever met. "Little does she know," I thought. I cherished the opportunity with Janis to voice *all* my feelings, not just the rosy ones.

Janis also made me laugh; the Queen of Silliness had a knack for lightening my moods with humor. She sprinkled our conversations with a thousand funny stories from her past. In one of my favorites, from a restaurant job where she'd been required to punch a time clock, two coworkers who were dating fought by leaving notes on each other's time cards. Janis saw a note the guy wrote to his girlfriend that said, "Bicth, you anit no good!" Because of the spelling errors, Janis pronounced it, "BIK-thuh, you a-NIT no good." She found opportune times to spring that on me to make me laugh or just playfully call me "bik-thuh."

To cheer me up, she also recited, out of the blue, silly verses she wrote when we were best friends in junior high and high school. I welcomed the comic relief. In addition, having just lost someone who had witnessed my childhood, I drew comfort from Janis's reminders of my much-younger self.

Terry, a good pal from graduate school, was also able to accept whatever I was feeling with no judgments or "shoulds." Other friends, as well, made it clear that they were beaming love at me. They didn't treat me as though I had the plague because I brought death closer to their conscious awareness. I gratefully received all demonstrations of caring and compassion, large and small.

Despite the outpouring of support I received from friends, much of my pain was too great to take anywhere besides therapy. So many issues, both old and new, were unearthed by my father's death that I often felt like a bottomless pit—an excessive level of need to take to a friend. That magnitude of pain belonged either in the realm of the spiritual ("Turn it over to God," the twelve-step programs say) or in therapy. Trying to secure enough support from friends to fill the inner void caused by a major loss seemed fraught with hazards and destined to create imbalances that would be difficult to heal later on. Blessed with a wide range of loving support, I learned what I could ask of friends and what to take into my work with Paul.

CHAPTER 12

Accepting Death

Much of my shock over losing my father was related to facing death for the first time. My grandparents all died before I was born or when I was very young. My father's first wife's parents, whom we had included in our family gatherings, died several years before my father, but I wasn't close enough to either of them to feel their passing as a personal loss. I'd known several young people who died in their teens, including Janis's brother, but hadn't felt strong ties with any of them.

Losing my father was different. I had to face the raw reality of never seeing him again, of his tremendous vitality being gone—not only from my life but also from the world. As my first close-in experience of death, it had great impact, a feeling of emptiness I will know for the rest of my life.

I recalled that feeling four years later when Dan, the father of my then-partner, Bruce, died suddenly of an asthma attack. Bruce and I drove from Santa Fe, New Mexico, to Sierra Vista, Arizona, to make funeral arrangements, and again two weeks later to empty out Dan's mobile home. In a frenzied ten-hour yard sale, his possessions—almost all tangible evidence of his life—morphed into a fanny pack full of money. How could a life disappear like that?

Since my mother continued to live in the home she and my father had shared, concrete evidence of his rich life remained: his music books, his brown tweed recliner, his office adorned with music posters and a framed concert program autographed by David Oistrakh. I frequently flipped through the pages of the red leather address book in his middle desk drawer, comforted to see his strong, distinctive handwriting. My mother gave me several of his possessions—a bright blue summer jacket, his burgundy terry cloth bathrobe, a ceramic cereal bowl he'd used daily, a gray soapstone dish that had held his pocket change. I particularly treasured things he had handled frequently, imagining that I could still sense an imprint of his energy.

～

After my father's cremation, we received a generic cardboard box with a typed label stating that his ashes were contained therein. The box sat on a shelf in my mother's living room closet during the four months I lived with her after his death. Every time I went into the closet, I winced at the thought that a cardboard box measuring six by six by eight inches held all that remained of my father's physical body. I avoided the closet, not wanting the graphic reminder of the destruction of his beautiful face and form. My shock and fear turned the box into a haunting presence.

In keeping with my father's wishes, my family intended to scatter his ashes in the river by the valley home where my parents had lived. A ceremony was planned for the one-year anniversary of his death, by which time I planned to be back in San Francisco. As the months passed and the time of my departure neared, I knew I had to open the box and look at my father's ashes before leaving, both to bid a final farewell to his physical form and as another step in facing the reality of his death. Opening the box terrified me. Finally, the day before I left for San Francisco, I forced myself to take it down from the shelf.

I used to work in the field of archaeozoology, and my work included identifying animal bones from archaeological sites. This work required a thorough knowledge of skeletons, including an ability to recognize individual bones and identify them from small fragments unearthed at sites.

Looking at my father's ashes was even more shocking than I'd anticipated. I hadn't known I would be seeing identifiable bone fragments mixed in with the powder. I was horrified not only to absorb the reality of my father's strong, animated form reduced to a box of lifeless material, but also to be able to identify actual fragments of vertebrae and limb bones. I sat for forty-five minutes in utter bewilderment, wanting to flee yet riveted, knowing I had to face the truth I wanted so much to deny.

Two weeks later I had a dream:

> *I'm sitting in a potter's studio, and on the wheel I see a large pot that has been thrown and is still wet. Something beckons me to come closer—a voice, or a knowing, that inside the pot are my father's ashes. There is no horror or hesitation. I feel an organic kinship with the wet, live clay; I want to touch it and be close to it. I approach the pot, reach inside, and feel not my father's dry ashes but instead his tangible energy, his consciousness and essence, merged with this very alive material from the earth. I feel tremendous peace, like holding bread dough that is warm and risen—a comforting, nourishing, organic whole.*

> *I realize that my father is not just his discrete body, which was destroyed, but is also a vibrant energy that left his physical form and is now merged with the earth, the wind, with life itself. I know that everything is okay, that this pain will pass, that he is everywhere and with me. I'm not as afraid anymore.*

While living with my mother, I thought about the difference between losing a parent and losing a spouse. My mother and I talked about this from time to time with no thought of whose pain was worse. We each had our own experience and emotions, and perhaps because our vantage points differed, we were able to offer each other extra support.

I knew, of course, that she was losing the primary person in her world, and each day for the remainder of her life she would feel his absence. I'd lived my adult life mostly solo up to that point and had never opened myself to true intimacy with a romantic partner. I was unable to fathom the pain of losing a life partner of more than forty years.

I helped her adjust to being alone, which was my specialty. For years I had delighted in the sense of accomplishment I derived from being independent. Because mainstream culture promotes the myth that a woman is incomplete without a man, each step toward my self-sufficiency and competence had been a source of pride, particularly in areas where women weren't expected to excel. So when I drove cross-country alone, changed a car headlight, or solved a mechanical problem, I felt I'd accomplished something significant.

My mother, who'd lived an adventurous single life in her twenties, had fallen out of the practice of independent living. As the wife of a take-charge man who handled many tasks, particularly those falling along traditional male lines, she had been shielded from much of the joy of autonomy. Now with him gone, she faced problems with meager experience to draw on. "What do I do when a neighborhood kid knocks down the mailbox?" she wondered. "How many things about the car need regular attention?" "Can I really drive to Washington, D.C., by myself?" In the early stages of grieving, each of those challenges was a burden, another reminder that her husband was gone, and with him essential support she'd relied on for decades. As she continued to grieve and heal, she began to discover the delight that accompanied tackling those tasks. When she went "tootin' off" to Washington by herself and relished the freedom of being alone on the road, I knew she'd rediscovered the joys of going solo. Not that she would choose them over the joys of a twosome—they were different joys—but if circumstances forced her to be alone, she'd survive more easily if she allowed herself to experience the delights and not just the pain.

Losing my father was quite a different matter. He hadn't been a daily presence in my life for twenty years. We spoke on the phone once or twice a month, and I visited once a year or less. His death was more about what he represented inside me, and I experienced long months of bewilderment and grief as I struggled to sort out the disruption to my internal world.

Losing my father represented losing a large piece of my history—his memories of me as a child, his experiences and understandings of my growing up, his stories about me. He was one of the most influential people in my development and certainly the most important male figure. From him I learned what men are about, as well as what I was about by seeing my reflection in him and in his responses to me.

He was there for me in many of the ways fathers are traditionally "supposed" to be, teaching me about life in the material world and how to keep it running smoothly. He taught me to balance a checkbook and drive; he explained insurance, retirement accounts, car maintenance. He paid for me to attend college and various academic enrichment programs. He sold me my first car while I was in college, banking my payments and returning them to me as a graduation gift. One day he sold an old life insurance policy in my name and sent me a check for $520.

My mother was my emotional support in the family, the comforter, the one who understood. My father was the materializer, a role more unconscious to me—not a consistent, loving presence, but behind the scenes providing solidity and security. Because my relationship with him had been so tumultuous and painful, I had grown to adulthood more focused on the ways he had failed me than the ways he had supported me. His death brought a sharp awareness of the grounding and stability he had provided, which, once conscious, triggered panic as I faced the void created by his absence. Despite the fact that I'd been self-supporting for years, a little-girl part of me cried out, "Who's going to take care of me?"

My mother consoled me as I worked through my feelings. It helped to know she had survived the loss of her parents. We talked about the circumstances surrounding their deaths, what was happening in her life at the time, how she felt, how she coped. We talked about the ways in which she made peace with losing them as well as how she felt decades later. She'd also lost important close friends, including Evelyn, a strong, independent role model who had encouraged her to follow her own unique life path. My mother demonstrated how a person lives through major loss and gave me tools for healing as well as the knowledge that some of the pain never goes away. Although the death of a loved one was always difficult, somehow the idea of it had become a bit less shocking to her. I needed to hear that—to know that each loss wouldn't be as catastrophic as the first.

My mother and I also talked at length about the circumstances of my father's death and considered better and worse situations. Certainly the accidental aspect made it difficult for us to accept. Whenever we hit on that piece, we felt so overwhelmed with emotion and helplessness that we often just put the topic away. Even my understanding that he had been psychologically preparing to die was meager comfort for the outrageous fact that someone's carelessness had caused him to lose his life and be taken from us.

She and I compared the eight weeks of my father's illness and death to circumstances of acquaintances and friends. Jake, a close family friend with Alzheimer's disease, had been deteriorating for years. Rae, his wife—a widow with a living husband—suffered

horribly as she watched his growing debilitation and faced the in-
evitability of his death. In addition, for years she bore the burden
of being his primary caretaker. My mother and I were thankful
that my father didn't linger in a state of degeneration and suffering that robbed him of dignity.

We also discussed people whose deaths were instantaneous and
whose families had no time to say goodbye or prepare emotionally. Catherine Ellsworth, the neighbor mom in Ashtabula, died
suddenly of complications from diabetes three days after my father died. (My mother and I joked that wherever those two were
headed next, everyone around them had better look out because
they were feisty as all get-out.) We were grateful that the time
frame of our situation allowed us to process emotions in preparation for my father's eventual death, affording us an opportunity
for closure and for taking the first steps toward acclimating to his
absence. Even in the midst of our pain, we saw that things could
have been much worse.

～

Three years after my father's death, I interviewed his sister,
Rose, to learn more about his childhood and family background
as part of my research for this book. While recalling the deaths
of other siblings, all older brothers, she began thinking about my
father's coma. She shared the following:

> *I just couldn't face the fact that he wasn't going to wake up.
> Every day I'd go to the hospital with renewed hope. And for a
> while I was so encouraged because when Uncle Bill [her hus-
> band] and I were alone with him, I was holding his hand and
> I said, "Lou, if you can hear me, squeeze my hand," and he
> squeezed it, and Uncle Bill was right there and he saw. And I
> said, "Squeeze it again, but squeeze it hard," and he squeezed
> my hand so hard. And we did it about two or three times, and*

he heard me. And I said, "So Lou, wake up! Open your eyes!"
And he raised his eyebrows as if he was trying to open his eyes. I
was so encouraged, I was so excited. I came home and I quickly
called your mother, and I said, "I talked to him. He heard me."
I don't know who said it's a reflex, but it couldn't have been
because he only did it when I told him to. So I was hoping that
if I kept talking to him, he would wake up, but he didn't.

Hearing that story affected me in ways I didn't recognize for
weeks. But suddenly I found myself agonizing over the thought
that perhaps taking my father off life support had been a mistake
or at least a decision we should have delayed.

At the time, we heard the neurologist's assessment, confirmed
by other specialists, that my father would not recover a meaningful quality of life. As his family, we were certain he didn't want to
live in a vegetative state. The neurologist assured us that my father
himself had made the decision by signing a living will before his
illness. We gained comfort from realizing that our task was simply
to carry out his wishes.

After talking with Aunt Rose, I shared with my mother my
agony about terminating my father's life support. It was then that
I learned I'd been confused about some of the medical facts. I'd
understood that the staph infection affected my father's brain
function; I only learned later that after surgery it had festered and
grown, progressively destroying more tissue and any hope of recovery. So it was quite possible that Aunt Rose did elicit a genuine
response from my father, but that his capacity to respond faded
and disappeared over time.

I was baffled that I hadn't absorbed this information at the time
of his death. Perhaps I was emotionally overloaded to such an
extent that I didn't make the obvious connections. Understanding the medical facts would have allowed me to make peace with

the inevitable choice to discontinue life support. Yet not comprehending all the facts forced me to wrestle with deep emotions that were still with me years later.

To say "That's what he would have wanted—we need to discontinue life support" isn't simply a rational choice. My feeling side felt whisked through the decision-making process, not fully taking in the weight of making that determination for another human being. My nephew Danny, age twenty-one at the time, voiced the emotional impact when he heard the decision and commented, "You mean you're going to starve him to death." All the medical facts in the world couldn't counter the reality of making such a ghastly choice. Yet I didn't feel the full force of the decision when we made it. My perceptions were clouded by my pain, my wishes, my need for resolution. There came a time when any answer was better than none. Finally, I just wanted to make peace with the fact that there was no hope. I just wanted it to be over.

Perhaps my agony about terminating life support was simply a way to acknowledge later on how much I'd lost touch with my feelings after weeks of crisis. Perhaps the pain was a reminder that however appropriate our decision, it was never an easy choice or one that could be made without emotional repercussions. Or perhaps my torment was simply a way of facing, yet again, the fact that my father was gone.

My father's parents, Bessie (Bubu) and Joseph

Left to right: My father, siblings Morris,
Ed, Rose, and Ben, and their parents

My father and
his sister, Rose,
in 1922 or 1923

My father in 1928
at age eleven or twelve

My father as a
young violinist,
1930s

Left to right, standing: Ed, Ben, my father, Morris
Sitting: Bubu, Rose, 1944

"The boys": Ben, Morris, and my father, 1950s

Me, 1954

My father and
me, late 1950s

Me in August (left) and December (right) 1965, just before and after my fourteenth birthday

My father when he proudly graduated from high school, early 1960s

My father with his
beloved chain saw
and taking a break
from working on the
winter woodpile, 1980s

During our
European trip,
1978

My father flying a kite in the Ashtabula meadow and feeding seagulls on vacation in Florida, 1980s

Charlie and me

CHAPTER 13

Life Choices

In the weeks following my father's death, I spent hours digging through family photos for good shots of him to copy for family members. The photos immersed me in the energy of his aliveness, replacing hospital images of him helpless or in pain with memories of him engaged in activities that had brought him pleasure—playing the violin, cutting a log with his chain saw, feeding seagulls, proudly posing with a perfect loaf of bread he'd baked, playing with his infant granddaughter, and grinning in anticipation as he cut into a schaum torte, his favorite dessert.

During my search, I found a box of old black-and-white photos taken before my birth or during my early childhood. Mixed in were other memorabilia of that era—report cards from long-forgotten elementary schools, a valentine I'd made with a fat kindergarten crayon, and yellowed newspaper clippings about my father serving as a United Way campaign manager, my mother speaking to the American Association of University Women about her post-World War II work in Yugoslavia, Mark winning his fourth-grade spelling bee, and me finding a mistake in the *World Book Encyclopedia* dinosaur article when I was seven.

As I witnessed the accumulated history of my parents, who had joined their lives and created a family, I felt a rush of sorrow for the solitude of my own life. Looking back on my past, I saw that my intimate relationships were so short-lived that I never created much shared history.

For the first time, I let myself feel that loss. In the past, I'd simply relished my freedom and been unwilling to trade it for the limitations of commitment and settling down. Indeed, my life *had* been rich in adventures. I'd lived in seven states and traveled to forty-two. (In 2005, I fulfilled a goal of seeing all fifty states with a trip to Alaska.) I'd visited Scotland four times as well as Canada, Mexico, Bermuda, Ireland, Italy, and Yugoslavia. I'd spent summers learning French in Montreal, Spanish in Cuernavaca, active citizenship in Montana, and old-timey banjo in West Virginia. I'd studied animal bones at an archaeological research station in Illinois, spent five weeks on Hawaii's Big Island, traveled for six weeks in British Columbia, played folk music at cafes and festivals. I'd worked for a contract archaeology office in New Mexico, camping in the desert and searching for traces of prehistory. I'd volunteered with the United Farm Workers for six months at their California headquarters, including the time of Cesar Chavez's last fast.

I'd also done much inner searching, working actively in therapy on and off since the age of nineteen to unravel patterns created by a childhood of adaptation to my father's violence and my mother's overprotection. Therapy provided a place to observe my behaviors and question their efficacy in my life—my hypervigilance, self-protection, and reflexive isolationism. It also offered an opportunity for honest, supportive exchange with other humans, which was mostly absent in other arenas of my life. Over the years, I'd become increasingly brave about facing my demons and breaking through blocks to wholeness.

Still, I was addicted to a solo life. I grew as I followed internal promptings, unfettered by consideration of another's needs, schedules, demands. I knew the sweetness of living true to myself and making that my highest priority. The rewards were knowing myself well, being able to speak my truth, respecting interpersonal boundaries and honoring my own, and feeling relatively immune to what others thought of me. In addition, my formerly outspoken inner critic was mostly quiet, replaced by self-compassion and self-acceptance. This was the rich harvest of the life I'd lived up to then.

Yet every choice is a trade-off, and in following one path I'd turned my back on another. I looked around and saw people with companions, people who had forged their lives in partnership. As a young adult I'd felt excluded, wondering why others got to have something I was denied. Then I realized the obvious: just because they're together doesn't mean they're happy. And I could choose that path, too—only I couldn't. I'd come too far to trade my soul for security, to sell out for the companionship of someone who wasn't right for me. Many years earlier, I'd stopped wanting someone just to have someone.

But the grief that visited me as I looked through family memorabilia was much deeper than the issue of being alone. It was about the richness of building a life with another person—not just to have someone, but out of authentic love and respect for a partner and the desire to materialize shared visions. My grief was about the potential for intimacy that lay dormant in me—a desolation powerful enough to flatten me, keeping me in bed until noon for days. Every time I thought about that box of family history, I wept for a time in my life that would never be.

Again, some of this was by choice. I knew at age twenty-two that I didn't want children. I searched for years to find a doctor who would perform a tubal ligation, only to be told time and again that I couldn't possibly make that decision at such a young age. One doctor even had the nerve to suggest that as soon as I met "Mr. Right," I'd surely change my mind.

When I was twenty-nine, I finally found a doctor willing to perform the procedure. After examining me, he explained the details of the surgery, told me his nurse would contact me about scheduling, and then said goodbye and started to leave the room. Incredulous, I stared at him and asked, "Aren't you going to try to talk me out of this?"

He smiled warmly and said, "No. You're a grown woman—it's your choice. I assume you know what you want." In that moment I felt more respected by a man than ever before.

In the years since the surgery, I've never regretted my decision. However, several men in my life have been troubled by it. "You can get it reversed, can't you?" Richard asked early in our relationship.

I replied, "I don't *want* to get it reversed. I wouldn't have done it if I hadn't been sure." Any man who felt compelled to have children simply was not meant to be my life partner.

In retrospect, the decision to end my fertility had roots in both my pain and my clarity. The pain was tremendous anger at men— and women, I later learned—and an unconscious compulsion to withhold myself from them. "I'll never let you get to me," I'd vowed, which stemmed from my childhood, when withholding was the only way to retain my personal power. From my father I withheld my authenticity for my own safety. From my mother I withheld my warmth because she worked so relentlessly to draw it out of me to feed her own emotional needs. Although I've worked to heal from the effects of those early patterns, they have shaped my personality in profound and persistent ways.

The pain was also about the energetic sense of invasion I'd experienced as a child with both of my parents. My father's physical abuse and my mother's physical and emotional smothering gave rise to a fundamental desire to keep my body to myself.

The clarity about my choice emerged from several things: first, the simple fact that having children has never been part of my vision of my ideal life, and second, a frank recognition that I'm not temperamentally suited to parenting. I thrive on solitude and the freedom to follow my own inclinations. I quickly get frustrated when anyone demands too much of my attention or becomes dependent on me—surely a reaction developed in childhood, when my sense of agency was thwarted at every turn. As an adult, I've not been interested in putting my personal goals on hold for years at a time, as I've seen many parent-friends do. Since that lifestyle doesn't suit me, the benefits of having children have never outweighed the costs. I'm grateful to live in a time when having children is a choice and not an obligation.

Clarity also came during a profound afternoon at a Findhorn Foundation workshop. I learned a technique for resolving ambivalent feelings and making decisions that involved "trying on" choices in a meditative state similar to active imagination. The technique involved quieting my mind, imagining one of the options in as much sensory detail as possible, and simply noticing what came—images, sounds, feelings. After sitting with the impressions and taking them in, I allowed them to dissolve, recentered myself, and imagined a different option, again noticing what came to me. This technique was taught as an effective way to access my inner truth, bypassing "shoulds" and the agendas of various parts of me that might be at odds with each other. Eager to try out the technique, I chose to explore my tubal ligation, revisiting that decision to see if any unresolved emotions lingered.

I took a long walk and found a peaceful spot to meditate. After taking deep, regular breaths for several moments to still my mind, I asked for a sense of my life without children. I felt a wave of sadness about not knowing the richness of that experience. After sitting with the feelings for a few minutes, I emptied my mind again and asked for a sense of my life if I *did* have children. The emotion that washed over me, much stronger than the earlier sadness, was an overwhelming sense of loss and tragedy. In that moment I knew that having children would prevent me from doing important work—that something significant would be lost. The feeling was so unexpected and unpremeditated that I trusted it, as I'd come to trust other strong intuitions. Since that time, I haven't felt prompted to weigh my decision again.

As I looked through family memorabilia and reflected on my lone journey, I began to understand that what was customarily considered the "mothering instinct" was, for me, more accurately a "creating instinct." When I saw people pouring themselves into parenting, I longed to give myself to something with equal fervor. I sensed that whatever energies lived at my core weren't content to sit still—that I would always be fully engaged in my life, continually unfolding the next layer. I'd created a great deal of richness in my life of relative solitude, and much more sought expression.

In the midst of grieving my solitude, I realized that I was doing what many people would call "feeling sorry for myself." Because of my training in psychology, I've learned not to put those kinds of judgments on my clients nor myself. I knew my sadness was simply an aspect of me that I'd never before allowed to surface. I trusted that if given the opportunity to run its course, the pent-up emotions would soften and release.

The sadness did ease over time, and along with it went part of my grief over losing my father. I hadn't understood earlier that much of my grief wasn't about losing him but rather about my own aloneness. Losing him to death stirred up sadness about the times when I'd lost him to fear or anger and the distance between us, which had been a lifelong companion. Allowing myself to feel it fully, and even be flattened by it for a time, released something that had been locked inside me for decades. When it left, I was able to live with myself more peacefully. I discovered that I could allow my grief about my solitary life—I could say, "This, too, is a part of me" without denying the feeling or pushing it away. In some mysterious way, accepting my grief about my own life helped me feel more peaceful about the reality of my father's death.

CHAPTER 14

The Child Inside

My sister Rowan was responsible for one of my most important emotional breakthroughs during this time of loss. Both of us had grown up deeply affected by our father's rage and violence. Her anger was closer to the surface and her vulnerability more buried, while the reverse was true for me. Not surprisingly, during our father's illness I was more in touch with feelings of loss, sadness, and fear. Rowan, more aware of her anger, taught me a great deal about accepting my own.

After our father's surgery, Rowan said she felt relieved that he was comatose because he couldn't hurt her anymore. Her comment shocked me, but I later realized I felt the same way. I also saw that however those feelings looked to outsiders, they were perfectly natural given the climate in which we had been raised. We each had a little-girl part of us who was still angry and afraid of getting hurt. Those parts of us didn't magically go away when we grew up; unless we helped them heal by working through and releasing the anger, fear, and sadness, they would continue to be tormented.

The relief I felt that my father could no longer hurt me lived side by side with my other emotions. My adult self was grieving the loss of more time with him and all the things he would never experience with us—weddings, graduations, new grandchildren, celebrations, accomplishments, day-to-day joys. In addition, I felt anguish about the violations inflicted on his body and spirit by this illness. Yet my little-girl part still felt safer than ever before, knowing I'd never again see his eyes ablaze with fury or his arm tensed, threatening to strike. I was thankful that my work in therapy and Rowan's wise support had freed me to say, "Yes, this is a part of me" without feeling guilty or whitewashing my feelings.

Months after my father's death, I attended a bereavement support group in which the facilitator mentioned that people often have difficulty sleeping after losing a loved one. I had to laugh—I was sleeping better than ever before, feeling safer in the world, no longer haunted by fear of my father's rage. Similarly, I began to sense a softening in my relationship with my body. Up to that point I'd hated exercise, never managing to sustain a fitness program for long without either injuring myself or losing interest.

Children who grow up in a climate of abuse often live in a state of perpetual terror. Over time, lacking the freedom to remove themselves from the danger and release that terror, it turns into body armor: shallow breathing, clenched jaw, chronic muscular tension, an inability to relax. When combined with dissociation, or cutting off, from one's body—another common consequence of abuse—the net result is that adult survivors often unconsciously treat their body as something to drag around or ignore rather than as an integrated aspect of themselves.

At age eleven, I gently awakened my father from a nap and he kicked me—hard. I never forgot, even though he said he was half asleep. I also never forgot the fury in his eyes, being struck or whipped for no reason, his huge hands throwing me across the living room. I learned well to protect myself, not only from him but from the world. I assumed a curled-up posture, which was both a symbolic expression of my self-protective stance and a literal description of the hunched way I carried myself. Exercising and standing erect required being physically open, vulnerable to dangers. Curled up in a ball, I was much less likely to be hurt.

After my father's death I began to feel drawn to exercise, not from an abstract conviction that it was good for me but rather from my body saying, "Please give me what nourishes me. It's safe now." This unexpected shift signaled that I had indeed shed some of the effects of my painful childhood and was moving on.

~

For months after my father's death, I was tormented by hospital memories of the week before his surgery, particularly times when he was in emotional or physical pain. Two incidents stood out: the moment when he stiffened and grimaced in great pain, prompting tests that indicated surgery was necessary, and the night he was placed in restraints and humiliated by the night nurses. Recalling those two incidents brought on intense anxiety similar to a panic attack.

I was also haunted by an image that came to me during his coma: a tug-of-war with him holding one end of the rope and the rest of the family holding the other. I sensed that when he died he let go of the rope, leaving us spinning in space, no longer grounded or balanced.

One day in San Francisco, I drove to the ocean and walked along the beach. After I lay down in the dunes and cried for a while, an insight came to me. I was reading a psychology book that discussed the concept of introjection, a process in which a person unconsciously internalizes aspects of significant people. I realized that my father had always represented being in control because it seemed to me as though he succeeded in every endeavor he undertook. To see him suffering, humiliated, and in pain disturbed the internalized image of him that I had come to rely on. Without it, I felt as though I was spinning in space without an anchor. I saw that, over time, I'd need to disengage from the introjected image of him as the one in charge and learn to rely on myself for that.

Losing my anchor also forced me to face the ways in which I wasn't, and never could be, in control. Facing death was in large measure about confronting the fact that many things in life were completely beyond my control and comprehension. There was nowhere to go with that, no way to get back to feeling good. Nothing to do but sit with the feelings and remember to breathe.

⁓

I use art therapy on a regular basis to give voice to my child-self. Art therapy has nothing to do with artistic talent. It's about the process and inner experience, not the result. Art therapy is a powerful tool for bringing awareness to symbols that reside in the unconscious mind. Giving expression to these symbols can provide insight into aspects of self that seek consciousness. The impulse may be to draw a house on fire, a tangle of brown and black lines, or a self-portrait with two heads. The art may or may not be accompanied or followed by a cognitive understanding of its meaning. Either way, the process can be healing by giving voice to an aspect of the self in a safe environment and may open the door to further engagement with inner symbols at a later date. It also allows energy to be released from the body through manipulating the art materials, which can be a surprisingly vigorous activity.

I learned about art therapy in a Findhorn Foundation workshop two years before my father's death. It provided me with a new way to give expression to my inner world. When I felt powerless about growing up at his mercy, I drew myself as a small red puddle of pain on the floor, shaded lightly to indicate my fear and my desire for invisibility to escape being targeted. I drew my father, ten times larger, in bold red and black lines to indicate his rage and his formidable presence. I added a child's scrawl in tiny letters: "I'm scared. Please don't hurt me. Just let me go back to my room."

After drawing many similar pictures over time, I spontaneously started drawing pictures in which *I* was the huge, scary person—

with big biceps, to boot—and my father was small, powerless, quivering. I was beginning to express my inner rebel, a formerly suppressed part of me that was angry and wanted to stop being a victim. I was also expressing a vengeful part of me that wanted to subject my father to the kind of terror he'd forced me to endure. My adult self didn't really want him to suffer, but I needed to give that other part a voice to acknowledge my desire to let him know about the pain he had caused me.

I continued to use art therapy during my father's illness and after his death. I drew pictures of him comatose in his ICU bed. In an early drawing, soon after his surgery, I wrote, "My daddy is sleeping and healing." As it became clearer that he wouldn't recover, pictures emerged in which I chased him across a vast expanse of empty land—I a tiny, helpless girl and he an airborne wind creature floating away like an escaped kite.

Many of these pictures came from parts of me that were in distress. The more I gave voice to them, the more I uncovered clues and released pain. Even though chronologically I was an adult, many of my emotional responses were guided by parts that developed during my childhood. Returning to those times and giving expression to those aspects of me was deeply healing. I released internal blocks by simply acknowledging, "This is what I'm feeling right now. It doesn't need to make sense, and I'm not necessarily going to act on it, but it's part of me." No longer did the terrified, angry, or helpless child inside have to keep hiding or go to her room and stay there until she was ready to be good; finally she was welcomed and heard. As I established a relationship with those parts of me, they relaxed, matured, and became more integrated into my personality. As a result, they had less potential to hijack my life.

～

I stayed with my mother while my father was ill prior to surgery and during his coma. My sister Rowan, a massage therapy student on a limited budget, wanted to move in. Every time the subject came up for discussion, I was gripped with an overwhelming anxiety I couldn't identify. My survival-level panic felt out of proportion to the issue at hand.

One evening it became clear to me. With uncanny accuracy, the entire scenario was mimicking a traumatic event in my childhood and triggering unexpressed emotions from that earlier time.

Rowan was born in mid-August of 1956, weeks before I started kindergarten. Prior to her birth, I was the baby of the family. This was not the preferred status one might imagine, not in a large family with so many diverse needs. I felt lost in the shuffle most of the time, ignored or dominated by all the bigger people around me. Nevertheless, I attributed whatever security I did have, whatever hope of getting my needs met, to being the youngest. When Rowan was born, my special status passed to her. From that point on, I felt discarded.

Two weeks later I was to start kindergarten, which I dreaded. Shy and sensitive, I was terrified to be alone among strangers, separated from my home and family.

The day of reckoning dawned. My mother stayed home with her new little baby—the one who replaced me as her favorite, my child-mind said—while my father took me to school. I screamed, I fought, I wailed. After gently trying to part from me, my father, at his wit's end, asked the teacher how to leave me. She told him simply to say goodbye and walk out the door. I felt utterly distraught, imprisoned in an alien environment full of strangers.

This scene replayed in my emotions when my father was dying. Rowan was about to take over "my territory" by moving in, and my father was leaving me, this time forever. The feelings had nothing to do with my adult self who knew that my father wasn't abandoning *me*, that my mother wasn't choosing Rowan over me, that Rowan wasn't taking my place. This was about a part of me, locked away in silence and helplessness since age five, now stirred to waking by a current scene that echoed the past in a mysterious, compelling way.

An internal voice admonished me for losing touch with reality and my adult self. I recognized this voice as one of the messages of a culture that encourages people to deny feelings, push through the pain, "take it like a man." A deeper place inside prompted me to open to the feelings and allow them to surface in order to be healed. It wasn't a matter of rationally choosing between the two voices—the wave of emotion was so strong that I would have been hard-pressed to stop it. I might have retreated to my room to shake in fear and terror until I buried the feelings again, but I surrendered to them, knowing this was an opportunity to release a piece of the past that had held me hostage.

Sitting with my mother, I began to talk about the panic. I told her that some intense childhood pain was coming up—that Dad was leaving, Rowan was moving in, and there wouldn't be a place for me in the family anymore. I began to weep, feeling the agony of the five-year-old "me" who thought she would be lost forever in her aloneness.

My mother, bless her, knew exactly what to do. She didn't try to reason it out with me; she knew a five-year-old child was talking, and that child needed her mom. She held me, rocked me, stroked my hair, told me all the things I needed to hear back when the original event took place. "I'm not going to leave you ... I'm right here ... You're my little girl and I love you ... Nobody's going to take your place." In those moments, that child part of me finally got the reassurance it needed.

⌇

For most of my life, I felt weighed down by a sense of isolation and a feeling that I was unwelcome in the world. My vitality was squelched by the feeling that I was an outsider. When I learned in my twenties that I had been an unplanned child and that my parents had initially been ambivalent about the pregnancy, that information became a metaphor (or perhaps an actual explanation) for my feelings of isolation. As well, growing up in an abusive home where my sensitive nature wasn't honored shaped my sense of being unwanted and uncherished.

Years earlier in a Findhorn Foundation workshop, I was feeling upset about being unwanted, certain that I had absorbed some of my parents' prenatal ambivalence about me. In the workshop, the idea came to me to do a sort of group active-imagination exercise. I had participated in an ongoing psychodrama group years before, so I knew the power of "rewriting" a piece of one's life. These rewrites can open the door to healthier emotions, new behaviors, and greater empowerment.

Group active imagination uses role-playing to explore a problem or issue raised by the protagonist in the scene. He or she sets the stage by explaining the central issue to group members and then choosing individuals to play various roles. A director helps guide participants through the scene, keeping the focus on the central issue and ensuring that ground rules, such as maintaining basic respect, are honored. The action is a spontaneous group enactment guided by the protagonist's goal of achieving insight and healing as well as the group's ability to identify with universal themes, which gives the drama a life of its own. Group members often play roles that allow them to express and heal aspects of themselves as well. Participants have the opportunity to practice new, more effective behaviors in a supportive environment. A deep sense of compassion often arises as participants witness and experience their own and each other's strivings to become more whole.

In the workshop, I staged a recreation of my birth in which I was symbolically in my mother's womb, curled up in the middle of a circle of people. While "in the womb," I listened to my "parents"—two people I had chosen because I felt safe with them—talk about my impending birth. "We've been waiting for her . . . She's going to be so special . . . We're going to love and cherish her . . . We want her in our lives . . ." Others in the circle said more general things: "We welcome her with love and blessings . . . The world needs her many gifts." Nearing the time of "birth," workshop participants beckoned me into the world by gently chanting my name. As soon as I was "born"—guided gently through a warm tunnel of people—I heard, "Oh, she's so beautiful . . . How wonderful to have her here with us . . . We've waited for her so long . . . We're going to love her and give her what she needs to grow into all she's capable of being." I felt loved, nurtured, supported, welcome.

After that experience, I felt less like an outsider. I realized I had projected feeling unwanted by my parents onto the whole world; it had been the only lens through which I'd been able to experience people up to that point. Being in the center of a warm, welcoming circle of people eager to contribute to my healing provided my "nobody loves me" little-girl part with a multisensory experience of being embraced. The group provided me with a new lens, a new template, a more positive way to see the world and my place in it. And while that experience didn't fully replace the voice of the outsider, it opened the door to other supportive interactions with people and also created space for tender exchanges between my father and me during his last days.

CHAPTER 15

Self-Care

Upon my return to San Francisco after my father's death, I went to therapy at least twice a week because I needed Paul's support to handle the onslaught of emotions that surfaced. Although I'd made great strides in learning to welcome my emotions during the previous two years of therapy, there was more work ahead. I felt overwhelmed, yet I knew this time provided a doorway into aspects of me that had been less accessible in the past. I threw myself into the turmoil of emotions that I knew promised to bring me into a deeper relationship with myself.

The feelings were a mixed bag of grief over losing my father, unresolved childhood issues triggered by his illness and death, and stress from the rigors of the hospital time. I had enough presence of mind to know that I'd navigate this difficult time better if I gave myself whatever I needed, so I didn't pressure myself to "bounce back" or be sociable or productive. I spent many days watching television, reading light novels, or curled up in bed sleeping. Often I was in such pain that I could do little other than cry. Sometimes the crying even felt good, and I'd invite it by looking at photos of my father, listening to a Vivaldi tape we'd played in the hospital, or rereading the poem my brother wrote and read at our father's memorial service. Because Mark's relationship with him was much fuller than mine, reading his poem allowed me to see our father through the eyes of someone who knew him well. My tears were for the loss of both my father and the opportunity to be close to him, which was now gone forever, at least on a flesh-and-blood level.

Post-traumatic stress, which I was experiencing, often manifests in flooding emotions and panic attacks. In my case, I associated it in part with having operated at crisis level for seven weeks. In perpetual emergency mode, I didn't attend to my basic needs, forgetting or just not having time to eat and averaging four hours of sleep per night. I also attributed the post-traumatic stress to the simple reality of facing pain that felt unacceptable, witnessing nightmares day after day without energy or adequate support to process my feelings. My adult-self and child-self had lived disparate experiences—one as super-caretaker, the other as horrified little girl. The situation was guaranteed to ravage my emotions.

In addition, I still carried significant post-traumatic stress from childhood. My father's illness and death fed into long-standing unresolved emotional patterns to create debilitating anxiety. I had a core belief—a carryover from childhood—that I wasn't going to get what I needed. Because the belief originated in an early survival fear, I felt that same level of panic arise when it was triggered. During my father's illness and death, that panic was just beneath the surface, unconscious and therefore unaddressed. Had I been conscious of it, I could have acknowledged that indeed I *wasn't* going to get what I needed—my father *was* going to die—but I also could have comforted myself better. The lack of comfort compounded the stress.

For months, any situation even slightly challenging, such as a broken pay phone, would make me want to scream or curl into a ball. Once I realized that this was post-traumatic stress, I found ways to nurture myself through the anxiety and regulate it. Sometimes that meant putting off unpleasant tasks or setting a limit on how many things I'd handle in one day, even if it meant canceling an appointment at the last minute. I'd pushed through so many feelings during my father's illness and death, overriding what my child-self needed so many times, that every subsequent time exacerbated the anxiety. The child inside was aching for gentleness and nurturing, and I was finally listening.

As I continued to work through my pain, I began to strengthen my observer self, the part of me that could detach from the anxiety and witness it from a calmer vantage point. I learned to identify when a childhood issue was triggered or when I was having an overload reaction that was a delayed response to the recent stress. Recognizing these reactions allowed me to not feel completely overwhelmed. I was no longer just the person in the water struggling to stay afloat; I was also watching from a safer place and therefore able to make clear, practical decisions about how to swim to shore.

Developing an observer self also helped alter my core belief about not getting my needs met. In therapy, I came to realize how profoundly that assumption had colored my life. I learned to identify when the assumption was being triggered, particularly in group settings when I withdrew and became numb. During my last quarter of graduate studies, I took a course in group dynamics—a theoretical exploration of how groups function and evolve as well as instruction in effective group leadership. Since the class itself was a group, it also offered participants the opportunity to observe individual and group behavior through the lens of the theories we were studying.

When I shared fear or anger in my class, I learned to observe my expectation that others would ridicule me or be indifferent. I was excited to be able to detach from that expectation rather than just be at its mercy. When I recognized the pattern, I reminded myself that I was now an adult who was able to take care of myself—by taking the behavior of others less personally as well as by maintaining a strong sense of self. Stepping outside the fog of my core belief also allowed me to notice when people *were* being supportive and kind.

Over time I made great strides in my healing, yet almost two years after my father's death I felt a place inside that was still in crisis and unable to move on. I didn't know what it was, only that it had a stranglehold on part of my vitality. It was a feeling unlike anything I had known, a crazy panic that came from holding terror so deeply inside that it screamed in private, muffled agony.

Finally the terror erupted. It was January 23, 1993, the two-year anniversary of the day I sat with my father in the hospital when he grimaced in pain, when the doctors discovered that the staph infection had burrowed into his heart muscle. I will remember that grimace forever. For me, it was a crisis more serious than all the others—the one when I steeled myself and said, "I'll be strong and get through this" even though I had no fortitude left. The following day was his surgery, when the staph infection traveled to his brain, causing damage that ultimately led to his death.

Anniversaries of traumatic events sometimes sneak up without forethought or expectation. It was Saturday, and I'd planned to do a few errands and then take a long walk in Golden Gate Park. But I awoke at 6:00 a.m. tired and cranky, and by mid-morning I felt a compelling urge to crawl in a cave and hibernate. Where was this coming from? Then I remembered the date.

Like most people, I'm not always in touch with my feelings or able to welcome them when they first appear. I avoid them, get busy, eat, sleep, fill my life with activity. But I can sense when I'm doing this because I feel a veil of escapism over my actions. After a period of conscious and not-so-conscious avoidance, I could no longer ignore the pull to go inside.

I sat in my bedroom with chalk pastels and paper, asking them to work their magic on me. I began to draw, prompted by the color my fingers wanted to touch and the movement my hand wanted to make. I drew a swirl of red color, then felt inclined to soften the edges of the swirl with my finger, spreading the chalk dust out into nothingness. As I caressed the edge of the color, something broke open—the poison knot that had been lodged inside for two years. No amount of comfort from another person could take the place of the comfort only I could give myself. In "comforting" the red swirl, I was consoling raw pain, a wound that, instead of being avoided, needed to be caressed, held, assured that there was someone to hold onto. At the time there were no words, just tears and more tears—for my pain, for the grave cost of being strong at the expense of my feelings.

Afterward, I came to understand that I had been skirting some of my most difficult emotions, fearing that if I surrendered to the pain it would never release me. Yet only by going to the core of my pain did I find the release I sought. I had been operating on top of the pain, like building a house on a shaky foundation. Only by slowing down, allowing the pain, and learning how to support it to heal was I able to make the foundation solid.

Cultural myths tell us that asking for help is a sign of weakness, that being tough and "having it all together" are more important than being vulnerable and emotionally honest. I often had difficulty setting aside those messages and listening to my inner promptings. But it was really the only road for me in my healing.

~

Taking good care of myself also involved lessons out in the world. Losing my father taught me a great deal about interacting with the medical establishment. My father had some outstanding doctors and nurses who treated him with commitment, professionalism, and caring. He also suffered at the hands of incompetent practitioners, from the ambulance medics responsible for his staph infection to the nurses who acted with unconscious cruelty by placing him in restraints instead of calling a family member.

Because the medical establishment in our culture has an aura of power and expertise, we're encouraged to put ourselves unquestioningly in its hands. Only after losing my father and repeatedly witnessing medical incompetence did I find my voice as a conscious person who deserves and demands to be treated responsibly.

A year after my father's death, I underwent a series of tests to identify the cause of bladder discomfort. As a hospital outpatient, I was to be catheterized so a clean urine sample could be taken. I was led into an examination room where a nurse appeared with a tray of equipment for the procedure. She donned surgical gloves, and as she began to prepare the items she coughed repeatedly, each time lifting a gloved hand to cover her mouth. I watched in disbelief as she continued the preparations with no awareness of what she was doing. As she finished and came toward me, I said, "Are you aware that you've been coughing onto the gloves you're planning to touch me with? You're *not* going to touch me."

She muttered defensively, "There's nothing to be concerned about" before leaving the room and sending in a different nurse to attend to me.

Two weeks later I was back in the hospital for a procedure in which dye injected into my veins was tracked through my body to determine whether my urinary system was functioning properly. The X-ray technician took several pictures, after which she excused herself to take them to the supervising radiologist for examination. She returned to report that the radiologist didn't think she had gotten precisely the correct angle to show what he wanted to see. She took several more X-rays and once again disappeared. When she returned, she stated that the radiologist still didn't think the angle was quite right, so another few shots were required. When she returned a third time with the same report, I demanded that the radiologist come in and position me himself so that he'd be assured of getting the correct angle. I made it clear that I wasn't a worthless test object but rather a living person being exposed to radiation. Lo and behold, the next X-ray gave the radiologist precisely the information he needed.

These experiences were my initiation into seeing through the passive mindset of "These people know what they're doing—I'll just entrust myself to their care." I learned to count on *myself* to recognize when something was wrong and to speak out against it. In doing so, I was challenging the "doctor knows best" myth that keeps most patients in a hypnotic fog.

I believe this hypnotic fog was instrumental in my father's death. He and my mother didn't have the conscious awareness to tell the ambulance medics, "Stop—you can't proceed with un-gloved hands." His death awakened my ability to trust my perceptions and speak up. I learned of my right to make informed decisions based on a partnership with health-care providers. I also learned to take matters into my own hands when necessary and to determine that I, not they, would have the final word on choices affecting my well-being.

CHAPTER 16

Conversations with My Father

After I returned to San Francisco following my father's death, my mother telephoned one evening to tell me she'd been crying and feeling sad and had sensed my father's presence in his favorite chair, a brown tweed recliner in their den. She felt an invitation from him to sit in his lap and allow him to hold her for a while. When she told me about her experience, I began to weep. I had also been sensing my father's energetic presence and offer of comfort. However, I'd been pushing it away.

Days later, I discussed this with Paul in a therapy session. I couldn't make sense of the fact that the very thing I had longed for all my life—tenderness from my father—was intolerable to me now that it was finally available. As we explored my conflicting feelings, I realized that in addition to longing for his tenderness, I also felt tremendous anger about how hurtful he'd been toward me. An angry part of me wanted to scream, "Why couldn't you give me that before?"

Exploring the conflict between wanting and fighting closeness led me to examine my suspiciousness toward men who were nice to me—I didn't trust their motives, didn't believe their intentions were pure. Because of my early emotional history with my father, I expected all kindness from men to turn into chaos and violence; I didn't know how to relax in the presence of tenderness or trust it to be constant. Paul explained that a tender, sensitive part of me had been frozen since childhood as a defense against abuse.

Thawing it out—bringing feeling back to that part of me—elicited pain.

Sensing an opportunity to resolve my conflicting feelings, I wanted to talk with my father in an active imagination exercise. Creative fantasy often helped me get to the heart of feelings and insights more directly than talking did. Paul agreed to facilitate active imagination in a therapy session with a tape recorder running. I lay down on the couch and closed my eyes, breathing deeply for several moments to relax and connect with a quieter level of myself. I soon found myself in a dreamlike internal movie with my father while at the same time externally aware of Paul's presence, able to hear and talk with them both. (In the following transcript of the session, the dialogue between my father and me appears in italics.)

Kira: It feels as if he's here, as if he's sitting here on the couch. And he's being really soft. He's saying, "I'm here to listen." I'm too scared to talk to him.

Paul: What are you afraid of?

K: That he's going to hit me.

P: Can you look at him and ask him for an assurance that he won't?

K: He says he won't. He wants to hear what I have to say. He's trying to reassure me. I saw him reach out to touch me.

[To Dad] *Don't do that. I've wanted that all my life. I hate you so much. I hate what you did to me.*

P: Can you tell him what he did?

K: *I hate that you were never there for me, that you set up a longing in me that's driving me crazy. I hate how inaccessible you were. I hate that the only contact I ever had with you was colored by violence and fear. I hate that I just had to go inside myself because I was so scared of you. I'm glad you're dead. I'm glad you can't hit me anymore. I keep thinking I don't have to be scared of you anymore, but I'm still scared.*

Dad: *I don't want you to be scared of me anymore.*

K: [Laughing sarcastically] *Well, what do you have to say for yourself? Why were you such a rotten father all those years?*

D: *I couldn't give you what you needed, and I'm really sorry about that. I really wanted to.*

K: *Why didn't you, then?*

D: *I hurt too much myself.*

K: *So why'd you have kids if you couldn't be a good father to us?*

D: *I loved you. You made me happy.*

K: [Crying] *Why didn't I ever know that? Why didn't you ever tell me?*

D: [Shaking his head in helplessness] *I wanted to give you all the things I never had, but I couldn't do it.*

K: *You made it hell for us. It was horrible having you for a father. It was horrible to live in fear all the time. It was horrible to think that nothing was ever safe because you were going to turn on us at any minute. I hate that we lived in fear all those years. That's not how to raise a family. It's not how to give us more than you got. You just did the same thing your father did. I wanted you to be better than he was. I hate what you did to me. I hate that you were always in my space. Now all I ever do is fight to have my own space, and there's no room in me to share it with anybody. You did that to me, and I hate you for it.*

D: [Crying] *I know I did that. I didn't want to, but I couldn't help myself. But I want to change it now.*

K: *I don't know if I want to be friends with you now. There's too much pain.*

D: *I don't believe you. I want to be friends with you.*

K: [Angry] *I just want to make you suffer for a while. I want to hurt you the way you hurt me. I want to be inaccessible to you the way you were with me. I want to be withholding. I really want to hurt you.*

D: *Go ahead.*

K: [To Paul] But it's sort of as if he's saying, "Go ahead and do what you have to do, but it won't hurt me." I was just wondering how I could really hurt him. The only thing that came to me was by hurting myself because he loves me—by living in that little space that he taught me to live in. That hurts him a lot.

[To Dad] *I don't understand. You taught me that, so why should you care? You created it.*

D: [Crying] *I didn't mean to.*

K: [To Paul] I feel really lost now. I don't know where to go.

P: I don't think he really did it to *you.* I don't think it was intentional maliciousness. I think he passed on what he had received. He had no conscious means of undoing it.

K: [To Dad] *I don't care. I just feel really angry. I don't care what the excuse was. You were my father. You were supposed to make the world safe for me. You did just the opposite. I don't care why. Everybody's got an excuse. I don't want to hear it. I just want you to be accountable for what you did.*

[To Paul] I feel helplessness in him, as though he's trying to make it better—he's trying to heal things—but I'm not letting him.

P: Right, because you're too mad at him.

K: Yeah—I'm having my revenge.

[To Dad] *Good—just sit here and feel helpless. See what it feels like for a while.*

[To Paul] And it's weird—he feels helpless, but it's not angry helplessness. I feel a lot of love from him, and acceptance, like—if I have to go through this anger, it's okay with him.

[To Dad] *What do you want from me, Dad? For almost forty years you completely drive me nuts, and then you want me to just forgive everything in fifteen or twenty minutes? You want me to just say, "You had this horrible upbringing, and you got really wounded, and you didn't mean it…" and I'm supposed to just be right here for you? Well, fuck you. I'm not just here to respond to your moods. And you know, it feels great to yell at you and have you just sit there. You can't take off your belt and whip me. You can't go pick up a piece of wood from the woodpile and threaten me. You just have to sit there and take it. You might have to take it for a long time. I don't feel like being nice to you. I don't feel like talking to you anymore…*

K: [To Paul] [Laughing] There's a part of me that says, "But this isn't permanent—this is just where I need to be right now."

[To Dad] *Don't go away. I'm committed to our relationship. I just can't talk anymore now.*

P: It's good that you're telling him that.

K: *Is that okay with you, Dad?*

D: *I'm committed to working this out with you, however long it takes.*

K: [To Paul] He's saying that as though he really wants me to hear him. He's really committed to me, and he can handle my anger. He's reacting to it—he feels things—but he's not going away. And I don't have to just respond to his moods or take care of him. He's just going to sit there and wait for me to be ready to talk with him some more.

[To Dad] *I'm glad you want to be that way, Dad. Maybe we'll get through this after all.*

D: *I love you.*

K: [Uncomfortable silence]

P: How does it feel to hear him say that?

K: I don't want to say it back to him.

P: How did it feel when he said it to you?

K: Scary—as though he really means it. He's not just saying it perfunctorily as he has in the past. I really feel his commitment to me. It makes me even angrier that I never got it before. But it's intriguing, too, because there's all this space in our relationship that was never there before. There's all this potential, all this room to move that I never had before.

I keep feeling the urge to be as scary with him as he was with me, to let him know how it felt. And then there's something inside that keeps pulling me back, like "Don't do that. Don't be that big. Don't take up that much space." I just got an image of him shrinking down to a tiny person sitting on the couch, and me standing over him screaming and him just curling into a little ball.

[To Dad] *Now you know what it feels like. Good. You just stay curled up for a long time. See what that feels like.*

D: *I've been that way all my life. I know that feeling really well.*

P: I think he does.

K: He's sitting next to me and he's crying, and he put his arm around me. I feel all this pain that both of us have carried for so long. We could help each other let go of it. It's as though he's not my father anymore—he's just another soul who's been in a lot of pain. We're two souls trying to help each other through some very painful stuff.

[To Dad] *I love you, Dad.*

[To Paul] It makes me feel so sad that as long as I'm really angry with him, I don't have to feel how sad it is that he's gone, and the minute I let in how much I love him, I have to face the fact that he's not here anymore. I mean, he is in one way, and I feel that, but I can't ever hold his hand or sit next to him or touch him.

D: *I'm right here. You have to believe that. Really.*

K: *I know you are. I wouldn't be doing this otherwise.*

[To Paul] I think he and I are going to be friends. [Laughing] I just got a sense that I don't want to make peace too soon ... like we're not giving in to each other. There has to be an edge to it.

P: You can't gloss over all the hurt.

K: Yeah, and there's still some power struggle there, and it's just going to be there for a while, and that's okay. I guess that's just all of my anger. I don't think he's angry at me for anything. I mean, I think his everyday personality was, but I don't think his soul is. I don't feel that from him. His anger was just his wound talking—it wasn't *him*.

I feel ready to open my eyes. Talking with him felt really important, very big stuff. I really felt him sitting on the couch, and I could see him, see his reactions and see the looks on his face, as though he was physically here. He wasn't making fun of me for anything—he was really listening. He wasn't trying to discredit my experience in any way.

P: He was fully able to take it in.

K: And able to understand why I have to work through this.

P: It's for him, too.

K: Yeah ... he never understood that before. He just thought I was stirring up trouble, trying to wreck the peace in our family.

P: He had no means of experiencing it. I can see what's in it for him to share this with you.

K: It feels as though so much of his life was incomplete and unspoken and unresolved—so much pain that he walked around with all the time.

P: I appreciate how you stuck with the process, stayed with the anger, didn't steer away too soon. Things shifted after you said all you needed to say. Did you hear the part about your way of leveraging anger against him is by staying stuck, staying in your box?

K: Being frozen is my expression of that anger.

P: The more you can tell him the truth and get at it consciously, the more choice you're going to have in your life.

K: I've always thought that being in that stuck place took care of something for me, but it always felt more like protecting myself. Now it also feels like revenge—active revenge. I never saw that before.

P: That's really important.

A week later, I made the following entry in my journal:

> *Many times I've thought about talking more with Dad, either with Paul or on my own. Occasionally I've sensed his presence and said hello to him, but I haven't wanted to talk. My desire to punish him is tangible, and I feel good about that. Not that I want to stay in that place—but I'm recognizing it as a part of me that I've never consciously made friends with before. I realize how natural it is to have such feelings after a forty-year relationship in which most of my emotional needs were disregarded. I see that I need to move through that angry place to get beyond it. It's no surprise that I'd want to have some control, some sense of power—and that I'd feel satisfaction in doing so. I feel good about having done enough inner work to be able to write this without guilt. I think it's natural to feel this, and it's so freeing to matter-of-factly say, "Yes, I've been hurt, and I want to hurt back" instead of being caught in the cycle of "He's dead—I can't say anything bad about him."*

I've heard about people deifying loved ones who have died—seeing only their good qualities and remembering them as though they were saints. I'm glad I don't want to do that. Yet the experience of Dad's illness put me in touch with his goodness and his gifts in ways I wasn't aware of before. I'm much more able to see his enormous contributions to my life and also more able to see qualities in him that used to be obscured by my anger toward him. I'm able to think of him with compassion—to understand the forces that shaped him and the pain he carried that prevented him from being the person he longed to be. Yet feeling compassion and appreciation for him doesn't negate the anger, the part of me that says, "You hurt me, and I don't like it!" I'm glad to be able to hold both sides without thinking either that the anger negates the love or the love negates the anger.

It's exciting to be able to explore this anger in the safety of therapy. My relationship with anger is being reprogrammed as I let it out in the presence of a man who accepts me, instead of repeating my childhood experience of expressing anger and having my bigger, stronger dad punish me, making it clear that he was the only one who had a right to be angry.

This experience is tremendously healing. It's allowing me to express things I thought would be with me for my entire life, and it's giving me freedom to move in areas of my life where I've always felt limited. Some of this is happening as a result of saying what I've always been afraid to say. It's also happening because my experience of my father in the hospital gave me a glimpse into his softer side. Having seen that, I can more easily imagine that he's capable of listening, caring for me deeply and expressing it, and stepping outside his own pain enough to see our perennial conflicts from a more spacious perspective than his ego.

Several days later I had a dream:

I'm getting married, and my father, an almost angelic pres-ence, is singing at the ceremony, serving as a channel for the purest, most sacred music.

I awoke from the dream in awe of having experienced my fa-ther that way. I felt great love for him and was honored that he'd visited me in such a sweet, potent image.

The following night I had another dream:

I'm in New York City at twilight. The neighborhood feels dirty and dangerous. There's an energy of furtiveness and a need to hurry in order to be safe. I'm outside the entrance to a large hotel. My father has just left the hotel and is fleeing through the dark streets. He's wearing only a pink cable-knit sweater, and he's schizophrenic. I'm chasing him through the streets, intent on catching him and returning him to the hotel room where he will be safe, but I know he'll elude me and that my efforts are in vain.

Upon waking, I was struck by the contrast between the two dreams and the feelings each one evoked in me. How strange to feel my father as a radiant, loving being and then to feel absolute craziness in him. I realized later that each of those dreams ex-pressed an aspect of my experience of my father—I knew him to be both inspired and erratic, unhinged, violent. Reminded again that my experience of him spanned both extremes, I could neither deify him nor brand him a monster.

The second dream also expressed my emotional turmoil over his death. I wanted to control the pain by returning it to a safe, contained place, but a deeper part of me knew I had to accept the dread as well as the lack of control.

The next day I felt drawn to talk with my father again. As I didn't have a therapy session for several days, I decided to try active imagination on my own, speaking aloud everything that happened and recording it so I could transcribe it later. After doing a breathing exercise to still myself and enter a meditative state, I was easily able to imagine my father's presence and converse with him.

Kira: *Papa, I'd like to talk to you. Will you come sit with me? Come sit on this side of the bed. Hi.* [He's sitting against the wall with his legs stretched out on the bed next to me.] *I miss you so much.* [Crying] *I think about you so much, Papa. It's so weird…you're right here, aren't you? Will you talk to me? I want to hear you. I want to be with you. Talk to me.*

Dad: *I just want to listen now.*

K: *I have some things to tell you that I could never say before. I feel so sad about how angry I've been all this time. I'm learning how to get beneath the anger, and I feel so sad that I could never do that with you.*

D: *But you're doing it now.*

K: *Yeah…I want you to hear this so much. I want you to hear how much I love you.* [Crying] *I was so angry all those years, and all I could tell you was how angry I was. What I really wanted to say was that I longed to be close with you. When I was a little girl, I wanted you to hold me. I wanted you to sit with me and hold me, stroke my hair, tell me about the world, help me feel safe in the world. I longed to sit in your big lap and feel your big, solid hands around me, helping me to be safe. I wanted you to hug me. And it hurt so much when you pushed me away and when you scared me with your anger and your violence.* [Crying] *That's all I wanted. I didn't want to change you. I didn't want to threaten you or hurt you or compete with you or win any battles. I just wanted to be close.*

D: *Let's be close now.*

K: *Yeah—I want that with you so much. Dad, just hold me for a while.*

D: *I'm right here.*

K: [Crying] *Just hold me. Just be with me.* [To myself: Let me feel this and let it in.] *I can feel you, Dad. I can almost smell you. I can feel your big hands. Help me heal, Papa. Help me feel what hurts so I don't always live stuck in the pain. Just hold my hands and help me feel your presence. Are you really here? Yeah, I feel you. I want you closer. Please come closer. Yeah, that's better. Let me feel you, Papa.* [Crying] *I miss you so much…*

What else do I want to tell you? I want to tell you about all the things I'm doing in my life. I want you to know me. I'm learning how to talk to people without being defensive and attacking. I'm learning how to be vulnerable. I think pretty soon there's even going to be space in me to have a relationship. I want somebody to love me, and I want to love him back.

I'm writing a book about us, Pop. I'm writing a book about all the things we went through when you were sick in the hospital and all the things I've learned. Maybe writing about it will help me heal and will help other people go through this with a little extra courage and understanding. I feel a whole world opening up for me because of this. And I feel so sad that I had to lose you to find this.

D: *I haven't gone anywhere.*

K: *What do you mean, you haven't gone anywhere?*

D: *I can see you right now. You look beautiful.*

K: [Crying] *I wanted you to say that to me so many times. I wanted you to tell me that you loved me and that you were proud of me. I wanted you to tell me that you respected me.*

D: *I was too defended.*

K: *Yeah. I longed for that person underneath all those defenses—the person who wrote all those love letters to Mom. I wanted to see that person.*

D: *I couldn't do it.*

K: *Why couldn't you do it? What was the wall?*

D: *I got hurt too many times.*

K: *Tell me, Pop, what hurts. Tell me what hurts for you.*

D: *I wanted to be held, too. I wanted to be safe somewhere. It was never safe for me. I didn't know about that.* [Crying] *I didn't know it was possible to create that for someone.*

K: *It's sad. You didn't even know it was possible. I wish I could have told you when I was six years old.*

D: *It didn't work out that way.*

K: *Pop, let me hold you. I'll stroke your hair, and you can cry for a little while. I want to give that to you. Yeah, it's okay to cry. It's okay to let out all that pain. I'm right here with you. Put your arms around me. Thanks. You're with me, too—I can feel it. I love you, Papa. I love you so much. I just want to rest here with you for a little while. I hope I can always feel you like this.*

D: *I'll always be with you when you need me.*

K: *I think I really believe that. You know, I was thinking last week about how the rest of the family is going to move on with our lives, and all the things you'll never see. Like you'll never see me graduate or find a partner. You'll never see Rowan have a baby—you'll never know that baby. You'll never see Joey* [grandson] *get married. You're so alive for us, but you're so gone, too. It's so hard.* [Crying]

D: *Does this help?*

K: *Yes, this helps. Will you really come talk with me when I want you to? You're sitting there looking so pensive. What's going on?*

D: *I want to tell you something. You've been a model of celebration for me. You've taught me a lot about how to live, how to free myself. I changed because of you. I softened a little bit.*

K: *Yeah, you softened a lot. I think I wanted to find a way to work some miracle with you, to dislodge all that. I wanted to be the wonderchild. I wanted to make it all better, and I couldn't. I wanted you to open your heart.*

D: *I did.*

K: *But then we lost you. You opened your heart, but you couldn't stay with us with your heart opened. I feel so sad that you never knew what it was like to be connected to us that way.*

D: *Oh yes, I did. I felt your presence. I felt you with me, in the hospital. I knew you were there. I knew you loved me.*

K: *You really did let that in, didn't you?*

D: *I sure did.*

K: *Did you heal some before you died, Dad?*

D: *Yeah…*

K: *I felt all the pain that was in your heart, Dad—and I felt it breaking free. It was like how the ice on the river used to break up in the spring—but it was as though it piled up and moved too slowly and it got stuck, and there was no way to warm things up and get them moving. But I saw it breaking up. It was so great to see you crying, Dad. I didn't want you to be in pain, but I wanted to see you soft. It was so important for me to see you soft.*

You can show me more of that now, can't you? You're doing it—I know. It's so funny how much I miss you and how much I feel you here at the same time. I'm going to say goodbye now. We'll talk again soon. I love you.

After that conversation with my father, I got caught up in everyday life for two months—finishing school, packing, storing my belongings in preparation to head east for the summer. Occasionally I'd feel my father's presence—a gentle tap on the shoulder, a request for time together—but I always brushed it away.

In the first months after returning to Cleveland, when the same thing happened, I had time, plenty of it, to talk with him. I no longer felt so angry that I wanted to punish him by withholding attention or love. But I was scared, pure and simple—afraid of the intensity of my emotions, frightened of the level of intimacy he and I had reached in our last conversation, terrified to be so undefended with someone with whom I had been at war for so long. And I feared feeling his pain, seeing him so fragile. He'd been my big, strong father for all those years, in facade even if not in reality. How foreign to see him vulnerable, limited in so many ways by the pain he inherited. How strange to see him as just another human being, lost and suffering.

As I continued to grieve and to integrate the insights that surfaced, my need for formal conversations with my father diminished. My anger and sadness softened and dissolved, and I came to feel a strengthening bond with him. His presence shifted from that of a tangible, discrete being with whom I needed to work things out, to a diffuse energy as immediate and benevolent as warm sunshine on my face. Nothing more to work out. I knew I was healing, not only from his death, but also from our long years of struggle.

CHAPTER 17

Intimacy

Bob Ellsworth—the Ashtabula neighbor whose wife, Catherine, died three days after my father died—visited one day while I was staying with my mother. They had a special bond born of having lost their spouses so recently and so close together. Raw with pain, they spoke of the significant growth each couple had achieved during their last years together. I knew of the peace my parents had found in their relationship, much of it attributable to Marshall Rosenberg's Nonviolent Communication trainings. Marshall teaches a collaborative approach to problem solving that de-escalates conflict and helps people listen to each other in less defended and more openhearted ways.

For years I'd heard about Marshall's teachings from my mother, who enthusiastically shared her insights with me. I'd seen visible results in clearer, less volatile communication between my parents. As well, I'd attended a weekend workshop with Marshall in which I acquired useful tools for my own life. So when my mother shared with Bob that she and my father had achieved a greater sense of peace with each other, I knew what she was referring to.

Bob's face clouded up as he said, "Yeah, you just manage to get to that place, and before you know it, it's all gone."

When I heard his words, anger stirred in me. I wanted to shout, "It's not going to happen that way in my life!"

As I considered my reaction, I identified two perspectives, equally true. On one hand, I believe that much of the purpose of an intimate relationship is for two people to join paths to learn deep lessons together. This happens all the time in marriages, whether or not the lessons are conscious. Partners painstakingly unearth their deepest fears and most primitive responses, ideally in order to eventually learn better ways to communicate, set boundaries, and allow intimacy. Perhaps when the lessons are exchanged—when the essential purposes in coming together have been fulfilled—the relationship no longer needs to continue in the same form. So, I pondered, perhaps my parents, as well as Bob and Catherine, had completed the lessons they'd come together to teach and learn.

Yet something else tugged at me to be acknowledged. In popular culture, marriage is commonly characterized, and experienced, as rife with bickering, sniping, and contempt. Couples who claim to love each other deeply often treat each other horribly, while romantic love is saved for extramarital affairs or for unrealistic fantasies used to measure one's spouse. Over the years as I've observed manifestations of the "battle of the sexes" with friends and clients as well as on television—a microcosm of our culture's dominant values—I've wondered how people in committed relationships who claim to love each other can feel and act out such enmity. Even couples who don't show animosity often seem to be subtly defending themselves against each other. Openheartedness and delight in each other's company seem rare.

Although my parents' marriage was not an overt battleground (nor, I presume, was Bob and Catherine's), a comment my mother made after my father's death gave me pause. She agonized over whether he'd been aware of the depth of her love for him. I thought, "After forty-one years together, she's not sure he knew?" I wanted more than that in a relationship.

Her doubt took me back to an exercise in a workshop on death and dying that I'd attended in my early twenties. Participants were asked to imagine being dead in a casket and seeing loved ones come by to talk to us at our funeral. As I relaxed into the visualization, I saw familiar faces and was startled to realize all the things I wanted to say to those people that I'd never allowed myself to express. My life changed dramatically from that day forward as I learned to say what I needed to say and no longer carried around a backlog of unexpressed thoughts and feelings.

After my mother shared her doubts with me, I spent hours imagining what it would be like to cherish another person moment to moment, to honor the soul-level connection in everyday life rather than couching it in defensiveness. I felt fiercely that this was possible—and that I would find a way to have it.

I wondered how my thinking and behavior would need to change for such love to be present in my life. What parts of my belief system would I need to examine and release? What assumptions about relationships did I hold that were at odds with my vision of true partnership? What automatic behaviors would I need to become aware of and find a way to dismantle?

Because I'd never experienced my father as emotionally nurturing, I grew up with no hope or expectation that a man could be supportive. I'd had numerous relationships, all fleeting, most of them with an inappropriate partner, neither of us open to or capable of true intimacy. I usually repeated the same dysfunctional cycle—choosing without much discernment, being unclear about my boundaries, getting into a codependent tangle, and ultimately returning to where I'd started: convinced that being alone was by far the best alternative. Then I'd spend long intervals of time by myself until a glimmer of hope lured me out of hiding, and the cycle would begin again.

Four years before my father's death, having ended another such relationship, I said, "No more!" I vowed not to get involved again until I learned how to be in a relationship in a healthier way. I theorized about what that meant but had no emotional capacity to do anything other than repeat the old pattern. Yet something had been set in motion by my declaration to abstain from a relationship until I could do it better. I was essentially asking life to teach me how to have a conscious relationship. I immersed myself in the question: "What must I learn to be capable of sustaining the kind of deep, intimate relationship I long for?"

The lessons came pouring in. Some of them came in therapy—having to face the ways I hid my vulnerable side from Paul and deflected human-to-human contact. After three years of sessions, including the period around my father's death, my armor began to soften and fall away. Not an easy process, but a welcome and necessary one.

I had much to learn with friends and family as well—hard lessons that I sometimes worked on internally and sometimes with others. I wrestled with whether to continue my friendship with Donna, my best friend, finally recognizing that she didn't share my hunger for self-examination. Our perennial conflicts were destined never to resolve if we couldn't explore them, so I resigned myself to ending the friendship. I struggled as well in my relationship with Kathie, particularly after our father's death when she criticized my grieving as misguided. Eventually I realized that she and I shared a precious bond, even with our many differences. I rededicated myself to honoring and nurturing our friendship.

As I felt myself readying for an intimate relationship, I still felt the shadow of my father blocking the way—the imprinting that remained from my relationship with him despite the work I had done. One evening during our father's coma, my sister Rowan and I shared with our mother that perhaps we needed to be free of him in order to have healthy relationships. At the time, I believed that his passing would release us from his shadow, which on a mysterious level may have been true. Or perhaps it was true because we believed it to be. But more accurately, we needed to free ourselves from the unhealthy patterns we had developed over a lifetime of living under his rule—both those he imposed and those we had adopted in response that now blocked our growth.

For me, that meant not letting fear dictate my course of action in a relationship. It meant allowing others to have opinions different from mine, neither adopting their opinion when it didn't fit nor being so insistent about being right that I invalidated those who disagreed. Kathie could love having pets and I could hate it—no problem! Just two people following their own likes and dislikes, not needing to convince each other of anything. What a novel idea, particularly in my family of strong personalities.

I also had to learn to speak up when I was uncomfortable or in need rather than hoping the other person would magically read my mind. And I had to make space inside for a true partner, not just an occasional companion I could discard when things became uncomfortable. I needed to give up my addiction to being alone. I recalled something I'd once read: "There is an illusion in the United States that a solitary life provides the greatest freedom. Most people don't understand that the greatest freedom comes from deep commitment."

One of the most significant obstacles for me to overcome was my sense of being unworthy of love. In part because my father didn't express affection toward me directly, I grew up lacking confidence that a man would find me desirable or love me. That was quite a hurdle to get over, and so freeing when I finally did. I attribute that piece of growth to my work with Paul—to little by little revealing my vulnerable self and experiencing the sweetness of support and acceptance. As we explored my isolation and its childhood antecedents, most sessions evoked tears, anger, or both. Paul not only accepted my emotions—he understood their source. I'd grown up pressured to suppress my natural responses to abuse and smothering: fear, anger, outrage, and a pervasive impulse to flee. Paul normalized those feelings and allowed me to express them in the safety of his office. He also helped me understand that I'd generalized the impulse to flee, believing *all* people (not just my parents) were unsafe. Together we worked to soften defense mechanisms that no longer served me.

A particular memory of my work with Paul stands out as a time when I learned I could be safe with another person. I was grappling with the issue of body image, working to accept myself despite the fact that my body didn't conform to the svelte cultural standard. Part of this work involved coming to terms with the body I had, so I asked Leila, a friend from grad school, to help me create a plaster-gauze mask of my torso. When the mask was complete, I hid it in my closet for several weeks; looking at it was too intense an experience of facing my embodiment, my overweight, my female form. When I was finally able to be present with the mask, I decorated it with magenta, turquoise, and purple tissue paper torn in freeform strips and glued to the surface. The colors helped bring a celebratory energy to my body, an emotion I didn't yet feel but hoped to invoke. As well, the care required to apply each piece of tissue paper felt like a nurturing meditation on self-acceptance.

When I finished decorating my body mask, I felt compelled to show it to Paul, wanting him to witness my process of learning to accept my body. I took the mask to a therapy session in a black trash bag. Paul and I discussed my difficulties in creating it and looking at it as well as my need to share it with him despite my nervousness. Then I took it out of the bag.

His first words were, "How are you doing?" That in itself was amazing to me—that he checked in with me about how I felt instead of just plowing through the task at hand. We sat silently with the mask for a time as I thought about the importance of learning to face the reality of my physical form. After a while, Paul stated gently that he thought the mask was amazing and powerful. He wasn't commenting on my body parts or my shape; he was commenting on the tangible expression I'd created of my desire to accept myself.

In showing the mask to Paul, I was able to move through my fears and get beyond them. But had I *not* been able to take the mask out of the bag, I wouldn't have been any less courageous—it simply would have meant that I first needed to work through other feelings. Growth in therapy isn't a matter of overriding feelings that stand between me and my goals. Growth is about having a safe place to explore and heal emotions that are restrictive. Each time I expressed my authentic emotions, I gained insight and expanded my options. And each time Paul compassionately accepted my feelings, he counteracted my childhood programming and supported my healing. Our work together was my first experience of a man honoring my emotions and my life in ways I could fully rely on. One of the major blessings of my work with Paul was to create space in me for an intimate relationship by healing my essential trust in men.

~

The Findhorn Foundation teaches a silent process, done in pairs, called "unfolding." One person assumes a posture that expresses pain, self-protection, being closed up. The other person creates a safe emotional and physical environment for an unfolding to occur, communicating an atmosphere of safety through gentle holding and soft touch. Then slowly, very slowly, the first person feels reassured enough to loosen a limb, uncurl a fist, expose the belly, let the body assume a more trusting and open position. During four months of staying with my mother after my father's death, I similarly began to unfold. By gently attuning to and honoring my daily needs, sharing deeply with my mother, and writing and drawing daily, I gradually released much of my panic and grief, and came to a growing sense of balance.

I had intended to stay in Cleveland through Thanksgiving but awoke one October morning with a sense that I should be back in the Bay Area by my birthday (November 18). Honoring that sense without knowing the reason for the prompting, I told my mother I would leave by November 10. I returned via a circuitous route, looping through the South to avoid ice storms and add the Carolinas, Georgia, and Alabama to the list of states I'd visited.

I arrived in the Bay Area the day before my birthday, settling into my cousin Judy's Berkeley home for a few weeks until I found a more permanent place to live. Judy was a great fan of the *San Francisco Weekly* personal ads, having met her then-boyfriend (now her husband) through them. She shared the latest ads, which I scanned indifferently—"thin, beautiful, passionate," they all seemed to say—until one jumped off the page at me. Had I stayed in Cleveland until Thanksgiving, I would have missed it.

ART IS LIFE—LIFE IS ART: I am average appearing, semi-Bohemian, vegetarian, positive, introverted, intuitive, feeling, perceptive, urban shamanic, cultural. I do normal job, performance art, primitive-experimental music, intuitive photography, spiritual-metaphysical living. I am 44, 5'9", 180, healthy not wealthy. I seek friend-lover for collaboration, grace, mutual invigoration and nurturing, our own zeitgeist.

The next day, I left a message on his voicemail, saying, "I think we have about a zillion things in common. Give me a call." Bruce called that same day; we talked on the phone for hours and met a few nights later at the North Berkeley BART Station. He had alerted me to look for someone resembling Elton John, for whom he was occasionally mistaken by strangers. Bruce had warm eyes, a ready smile, and stubby teeth yellowed from the over-fluoridated water of the West Texas town where he'd grown up. He wore the all-black attire of an "art guy."

At an Indian restaurant in El Cerrito, we sat across the table from each other—talking, staring, unable to eat, stunned by the number of interests we shared: left-of-center politics, health food, a persistent call to move to Santa Fe, a passion for cultural diversity, travel, art, music, wilderness, spontaneous living. Each of us had lived in many states, following a recurring impulse to seek new adventures. We instantly recognized each other as kindred spirits. After years of relationships with men who had tried to turn me into someone thinner, less self-aware, or more "mother material," Bruce's acceptance of me was on the order of a miracle.

His energy felt like a clear spring in which I immersed myself for comfort and healing. Over the next several weeks, I shared with him much of the previous year's challenges during my father's illness and death. Bruce listened without judgment or a need to analyze; he respected the fact that losing my father had brought into question huge issues around support, trust, faith—in short, had caused me to reexamine my entire life. He gently supported me through it all.

In retrospect, I realized that during my father's last months and after his death, comfort providers were in short supply since I was mainly surrounded by people as bewildered as I by what was happening. The biggest gift imaginable was to find someone who could simply hold me and allow my pain to be. I began to calm down and heal on a deeper level.

As Bruce and I got closer, my grief surfaced in unexpected ways. Opening my heart and learning to love intimately brought up fears of loss similar to the pain of losing my father—the terror of having no ground beneath me. What if Bruce changed his mind about me and left? What if he died? As I allowed him to become important to me, the fears surfaced time and again. I knew the feelings were intensified by my father's recent death, yet I also knew this was the risk of allowing myself to love. And it was all the more frightening because I had witnessed my mother's pain in losing her life partner.

I occasionally got angry with Bruce for not saying lovely, reassuring words to guarantee he'd always be with me. Life played a perfect joke on me by matching me with someone who wouldn't go through the motions just to make me feel safe. No, he was going to stare directly into the void and take me along in the process. So I learned about loving with no guarantees, no safety net.

As the bond between us deepened, so did my vision of a healthy relationship. I reflected on the notion, prevalent in American culture, that relationship involves compromise, sacrifice, and a fifty-fifty arrangement where, at best, we can expect half our needs to be met. The inevitable consequence of this thinking seems to be disgruntled people repeatedly agreeing to let go of what they want, convinced this is the best they can hope for and believing there is no alternative if they want to remain together.

Another common notion about relationships is that we are each incomplete until we find our "better half." Oftentimes, the purpose of this kind of relationship—whether conscious or unconscious—is to merge: to think alike, have the same tastes, go everywhere together. Marriage, then, becomes a process of slowly eroding each other's separate identity, with the goal of being duplicate halves of a whole and the payoff being to never feel the emptiness of being alone.

In contrast to this model of partnership, I realized that the long periods of aloneness during my formative adult years had been a blessing. I'd been free to grow into who I really am, learning to identify and live by core values instead of having my path detoured by the expectations or dictates of another. My experiences nurtured my vision of a relationship as a true partnership based not on compromise and sacrifice but rather on each person's freedom to nourish inner seeds and live true to self. A partner could serve as companion, lover, ally, and devil's advocate to share, support, clarify, and help sift out the obsolete debris.

My vision was not of two halves of a whole—it was of two unique souls retaining separate identities while delighting in the common ground they shared. Not that joining didn't create a new wholeness—intimate relationship added immeasurable depth to my life—but it worked better that we came together not out of a desperation to fill a void but rather with each already having contemplated the void, already in relationship with the void, so that we didn't each expect the other to make it go away. The void wasn't going to go away, and accepting that fact made it a third partner in our relationship that enriched us, both individually and as a couple.

I learned with Bruce that intimate relationship was much more delightful when everything wasn't already figured out. Each day was an adventure rather than a rote exercise in following a map, always knowing in advance where we would end up. Coming to this understanding, I began to see my experience with grief as an integral part of welcoming and dancing with the void. I had previously thought of grief in the narrow sense as the feeling response to the loss of a person, job, home, or life situation. I grieved when someone or something was taken away and I had no control over the event. I also saw that sometimes I made conscious choices that incurred loss; having been in a number of dysfunctional relationships, I knew that grief played a part in the endings even when I was the one who severed the ties.

I began to expand my notion of grief, seeing it as a useful tool in my relationship with Bruce. I had to grieve what I needed but didn't get, what I wanted that I couldn't have. In daily life I encountered many opportunities to grieve, and I grew as I learned to move through them. If I wanted Bruce to do something my way and he said he didn't want to, I had a choice to either grieve or try to control him. I could either require that he be just like me, or I could feel the sadness that existed in the gaps between us, the places in our lives where we didn't share or connect.

To do this, I had to acknowledge the part of me that wanted him to be just like me and see it for what it was: a fantasy. It's human to long for the reassurance that comes from knowing someone understands and shares my reality. But it wasn't realistic to expect him to be an identical twin, and any attempt to impose that fantasy on Bruce quickly disrupted our trust and intimacy. He wanted to be accepted for who he was, and he had a right to his preferences. Over time I learned to accept him and take responsibility for my feelings by grieving when I needed to.

I came to understand that intimacy wasn't a process of shaping another person to suit my tastes; rather, it was a process of two people with compatible needs and dreams learning to share and support each other in mutually nourishing ways. Intimacy required both of us to keep returning to the reality of each other rather than the fantasy. In every moment, I had the choice to either attempt to control him or to grieve the differences—feeling deeply the gaps between us—and only then to creatively work with him on solutions that took into account both of our needs.

~

Bruce and I were together for ten years. We moved from the Bay Area to Santa Fe, to Cleveland for a short time, to a horse farm in Washington State, and then to Seattle. We left the horse farm reluctantly, and I was filled with sorrow when I said goodbye to Shiloh, a pink-nosed white Arabian gelding with whom I had formed a close bond.

In Seattle, I found a volunteer position at a therapeutic riding stable, cleaning stalls and grooming horses on Saturday mornings before children arrived for classes. Two months after starting, I felt ready to handle Murphy, a Norwegian Fjord pony with the strength of an ox. As I led Murphy out to a paddock area, he bolted so swiftly that I didn't have the presence of mind to let go of the lead rope. I landed hard on my knees on rocky ground and was dragged for several yards before Murphy stopped at a fence. Just severe bruising. Or so I thought, until I tried to stand and couldn't put weight on my left leg. A searing, red-hot pain shot through my knee.

Emergency room X-rays revealed a broken bone spur on the outside of my left kneecap. Days later, an orthopedic surgeon further diagnosed a crush injury that had destroyed some of my already-sparse knee cartilage. He advised me to keep my knee immobile for several weeks and then begin a course of physical therapy. However, he made it clear that he held out slim hope for a smooth recovery. After a period of immobility, I began physical therapy, following every instruction to the letter and dedicating myself to my healing.

When my knee failed to respond over time, surgery became my only option. The surgeon moved my kneecap laterally, providing a new runway on which my knee could track. Recovery was slow. Four months later, I still walked with a severe limp and serious pain. When my healing plateaued after seven months, I continued to have limited mobility and considerable difficulty negotiating stairs.

I despaired of ever returning to a normal life and sank into a depression. How had my life come to this? I had a disabled parking permit and an assist frame on my toilet. Before boarding a Seattle bus, I had to ask the driver to keep the bus still until I found a seat, and I often asked passengers to stand so I could sit. My formerly active life was reduced to short, careful walks, frequent pain, and a constant need to coddle my knee. Few moments passed when my injury wasn't center stage in my awareness. I railed against my disability yet was forced to face it by the many tasks I couldn't accomplish alone or at all. My precious self-sufficiency was gone, and when I looked into my future, all I saw was a life of bleak limitation.

At the time I was seeing Roger, a compassionate movement therapist who offered a spiritual perspective on my challenges. One day he sat with me as I wept in frustration and hopelessness about my limitations. After several moments of silence, he gently said, "Spirit must really want you in a body."

"What did you say?" I asked in disbelief.

"Spirit must have plans for you that require you to be embodied. Otherwise, you wouldn't have to go through these challenges."

Roger's comments launched me on a quest for embodiment—to inhabit and live consciously in my body. I knew that I had dissociated from my body in response to childhood abuse. But it wasn't until I underwent surgery and physical therapy that I was forced to find my determination to recover my knee function and, by extension, my will to live in my body.

That quest ultimately took me back to my childhood, back to the terror still lodged in my cells about living in a body. If I became embodied, I would have to allow that terror to surface: terror of almost dying as an infant, of not being protected by my father, of seeing him change in a split second from Daddy to demon, of growing up with no one to turn to and the bleak emptiness of having to wait for years until I could escape the prison of my parents' home. The aloneness I'd lived with for the first two decades of my life still held me in its grip, crushing my aliveness and keeping me convinced that I didn't want to be here.

For the first time in my life, I was ready to go back into that terror. My time with Bruce had built a firm enough foundation of love and support that I had more inner strength to draw from. One day I said aloud, "Okay, I'm ready to face my abuse," and it was as though I moved into a new chapter of my life. I didn't realize at the time that the new chapter wouldn't include Bruce, but as I followed my process and kept taking the next steps to become the person I wanted to be, the energy between us diminished and flattened.

I went through a period of intense soul searching after Bruce and I split up, seeking to extract every lesson, every opportunity for growth. It would be simple to say he and I outgrew each other or that we grew in different directions—harder to admit that some facets of our relationship that we'd believed to be strengths were instead problems we weren't addressing. He and I shared many loving years together. We also avoided confrontation, playing our own version of the merging game, and it cost us. I often squelched myself, believing he couldn't handle the honesty, and over time I grew resentful of him and angry with myself for staying silent. He, too, avoided confrontation, and we ended up feeding a facade of closeness that eventually crumbled. We blew each other kisses from across the room and called each other "love," but we seldom addressed concerns head-on.

In addition, I yearned for a level of intimacy that he didn't seek. When I shared my growth with him—an insight about feelings, motivations, or family dynamics—he was rarely interested. And over time he shared less and less of his inner life with me. We reached a point where the connection was no longer salvageable, less from damage done by stored-up hurts than a bald acknowledgment that because of our differences, we no longer shared a common vision for our relationship. Six months after moving from Seattle to Tucson, we parted.

~

If my relationship with Bruce was like earning a generic B.A. in intimate relationship, being with Bill for five years afterward was a rigorous graduate program. My time with him was equal parts healing, purification, and wake-up call. I choose not to share details of the first two. The wake-up call had a lasting impact on my life, teaching me how to set limits with—and ultimately walk away from—toxic people. The emotional fallout from that relationship brought to my awareness the ways in which I still carried the legacy of childhood abuse. Although my relationship with my father had undergone a profound transformation, I was still carrying abuse in my cells, and I still acted it out unconsciously in intimate relationships. I hoped I could heal from that imprint, but I hadn't yet found a way to do so. Until I found the healing I sought, I didn't consider the story of my father and me to be complete.

During the time when I was grappling with the extent to which some of my old patterns—particularly my tendency to be overly accommodating with men—had resurfaced with Bill, I became intrigued with Internal Family Systems (IFS), a psychotherapeutic approach that offers an empowering, non-pathological understanding of human problems and a rich tool kit for practitioners and laypeople alike. I had a strong sense that IFS had something profound to teach me, so I signed up for a professional training and also began working with an IFS therapist. I wanted to learn the IFS Model by both studying and experiencing it, and I was in urgent need of support to navigate the onslaught of emotions that surfaced after I ended the relationship with Bill.

As part of that work, I spent time examining both of my long-term relationships. At one point, I realized that I chose Bruce because he was "not-Dad." My predominant relationship need at the time was to avoid repeating the intense, confrontational dynamic I'd experienced growing up with my father. I was successful in that endeavor, only to discover that it was strikingly unsatisfying. Bruce was emotionally detached—mostly unavailable for the quality of intimacy I sought—yet in need of a great deal of almost primitive contact. The relationship ultimately became dull and stagnant because it was driven by a need for safety on both of our parts. Placing safety above all else made for going-through-the-motions routines and a startling lack of depth. And Bruce's need for constant contact wore on me and clashed with my need for autonomy and space.

So what did I do with Bill? I chose him (at some level) because he was "not-Bruce." It's remarkable, in retrospect, to see the extent to which my choices of partners were guided by doing the opposite of what I'd done previously. I was bouncing back and forth between polarities, trapped in the extremes of my psyche. My vulnerability was shunned by Bruce; he didn't believe it belonged in a relationship, and sharing our psychological healing held little fascination for him. By the time Bill came along, my vulnerability was starved for acceptance by a man, particularly the kind of acceptance that, at that point in my life, I believed was only possible in an intimate relationship.

A young part of me believed that Bill could magically "make it all better" and provide a level of safety that could heal my pain, despite mounting evidence to the contrary. Thanks to Internal Family Systems, when the relationship crashed and burned, I had a unique opportunity to pull that notion out by its roots. Over time I came to understand that my higher self was the only one who could realistically provide distressed parts of me with the degree of acceptance, empathy, and constancy they sought. I'd had an abstract sense of that concept for a long time but never before knew how to do the inner work to make it a reality. With IFS, that became possible. I was finally able to clear out significant internal blocks and get solidly grounded in myself. My higher self's capacity to be a resource for any distress that arises has been expanding ever since.

CHAPTER 18

Meeting Charlie

Dream (2005):

> *I'm standing at the edge of an Olympic-sized swimming pool.*
> *A Native American man is walking on the surface of the water*
> *in the middle of the pool. As I look over at him, he reaches out*
> *his hand and says, "Come on in—you can do this, too."*

In the fall of 2009, after three years on my own, I started to become interested in being in a relationship again. Working from home, I didn't have many opportunities to meet men, so I joined an online dating site to test the waters. I corresponded briefly with a few men, but I quickly concluded that I wasn't going to meet the right kind of guy through the Internet. In fact, I was so unimpressed with the men whose paths I crossed in cyberspace that, after a few months, I let go of the idea of finding someone and decided to be content with my single life. Although I sensed that I'd been preparing for an intimate relationship for many years, and although I felt confident that I now had the tools to have a successful one, I had no idea where I was going to find someone who'd be a good match. I knew I'd need to be with someone whose values were far different from those of typical Americans. My number one criterion in a partner, particularly after my relationships with Bruce and Bill, was emotional literacy—a quality I've never seen in an online profile. I released the idea of finding someone while simultaneously turning it over to the Universe. If the

Universe wanted me to have an intimate relationship, it would make that happen. I didn't see anything else to do other than to stay open.

A few months later, in February 2010, I had a reading with a gifted psychic. After talking with her about career directions and other topics, I casually asked if she saw me ever having a satisfying intimate relationship. She nodded enthusiastically and said she saw me meeting my "divine right partner" on a walk.

The following month, I attended a Painting Experience process art weekend workshop that I'd organized. Process art, even more than art therapy, focuses on the internal process of making art rather than on the product, outcome, or meaning. The goal isn't to make a pretty picture or get to the heart of an inner inquiry. Instead, the goal is to simply let out whatever wants out, although it's not all that simple to get out of one's way and let it out. The format of the workshop over two and a half days created a meditative environment that enhanced the process. After doing several paintings on Friday evening and Saturday, I spent Sunday working on a large painting that seemed to have an "incubation" phase at the top and an "outpouring" phase at the bottom. At one point, I thought I was finished, but I asked the painting if anything else belonged in it. Bypassing my thinking self, I spontaneously painted two single-celled animals that were touching at one end and seemed to be befriending each other. Somehow I knew I was going to be meeting someone before long.

After the workshop, I set up a painting area in my apartment and painted on weekends. A friend from the workshop and I spent a day painting together. I continued to be entranced by the process of getting out of the way and letting the images emerge. In one painting, the single-celled animals had grown quite a bit more complex and were relating to each other more actively. And in the painting that followed, an embryo was growing.

I attended another Painting Experience workshop in May. During the workshop, I wrestled with some deeply troubling emotions related to an accident and injury, and late Sunday morning I felt as though I'd come out the other side. I started another painting after lunch that I finished at home the following week. While I was painting, I had no clue as to where the image came from. A whimsical and very pregnant aardvark floated above a watery world, with energy streaming out of one of its front feet and a burning bush hovering behind it. A multi-lobed organ in its chest was passing along an energetic charge to a group of swimming paisley shapes. As I looked at the painting, I intuitively knew that I was symbolically growing more chambers in my heart and incubating even more in my belly. Energetically, I was getting ready for something important.

About seven weeks later, in early July, I was taking my regular morning walk on the side roads near the apartment complex where I lived. Less than a mile into my walk, I saw a man up ahead who was taking photos of birds in a tree. I don't typically get friendly with men I don't know, but being a bird lover, I figured that anyone who was taking pictures of birds had to be okay, so I walked up to him and said, "See anything interesting up there?" We introduced ourselves and started talking as we walked. I knew instantly that Charlie was unlike anyone I'd ever met. He had no pretense, and I felt his authenticity as waves of energy traveling through me. We agreed to become walking buddies and enjoyed a lovely friendship for two months before it turned into more.

Charlie is half Native American (Island Chumash) and half Japanese. He's the man who came to me in the dream, walking on water, saying, "Come on in—you can do this, too." To my amazement and delight, I can. Charlie brings out the best in me, and my decades of work to prepare for an intimate relationship have paid off in spades.

Charlie's story leading up to when we met is equally incredible:

> *Looking back on major decisions in my life, starting with getting married the first time, having children, and buying my house—all of those were major decisions that I'd never thought through. I didn't get much guidance growing up, so I just did what supposedly the American dream was—get married, have kids, get a house. I had no direction in my life; I just did what I thought you were supposed to do.*
>
> *After my first wife left, I was taking care of four children by myself and having a difficult time of it. When I became a single parent, I decided that it was just something I had to get through for the next ten years, so I just put my head down as if I were in a storm and took one day at a time and tried not to think*

about the big picture because it overwhelmed me, and I probably would have given up.

I let the children know early on that I wasn't going to be raising them until their mid-twenties and that eventually they'd need to be on their own. I felt like I'd done my duty for the children, and I wanted to do something with my life that had meaning for me personally and that wasn't about taking care of other people. At twenty-five, I was taking care of a wife and children, and before I got married I was taking care of my ailing mother. I'd never really taken care of myself and done things just for myself, mostly because I didn't know what I wanted out of life.

So finally the time came to move out from the children, and I still didn't know what I wanted to do with my life at the age of fifty-one or so, and I really wasn't happy with the decisions I'd made up to that point. I had a feeling that this might be the last big chapter in my life—the last chance to do something meaningful—and I didn't want to make any mistakes. I felt that my life had been one mistake after another. I decided I needed to take a Year of Solitude to figure out what I was going to do with my life. So I got an apartment and made a rule to myself that there would be no girlfriends, that I would make no major decisions in my life, that I would focus that year on building up my freelance business, so that's what I did. During that time, I was able to focus just on me for a while, which was nice.

But as the year progressed, I still had no direction for my life. I really didn't know what I was going to do with it. The nearest I could figure, I was just going to wander around the United States with my freelance business, work from my computer, and be a vagabond. I started looking for where I wanted to live. I looked for places that were warm and that were close to nature but still offered access to grocery stores. I settled on Utah, but I still had no direction for my life. I honestly thought that I was going to die soon because it just felt like, if you have no purpose in life, if you're serving no purpose to the Universe, then there's no reason for you to be around. So because of that, I really wanted to have a purpose—I just couldn't find one.

So finally, one day, out of—I don't want to call it desperation; it was more a feeling of "I just give up," I guess, "I don't have any ideas, nothing's coming to me, my lease is about to run out, it's time for me to move, and I just don't know where to go"—one day at night, I was standing on the balcony of my apartment, and it came to me to just let go of everything. I mean, everything was up for grabs—my life, everything I owned, everything I was, it didn't matter to me. I just looked up at the sky and told the Universe, "I'm not using my life for anything valuable or useful, so I'm going to give it to you. I'm letting go of this life. It's yours to do with what you want. Just tell me what you want me to do with my life, and I'll follow that path."

On that evening, I didn't feel like, "I've done this great thing—I've made this great decision to talk to the Universe in this way." I was pretty forlorn. But the next day I felt a lot better. I was up at the crack of dawn, and there was this low fog in the sky, one of those fogs where you look up and see blue sky, and halfway down, everything below eye level is fog. Next door was an organic garden where people could go to pick fruits and vegetables. It was really peaceful, and I was on the balcony looking out over this quiet scene. When it's foggy, there's absolutely no wind, no noise, no birds, nothing. And as I'm staring out at this scene, all of a sudden one of those silver Mylar balloons comes floating out of the sky, and it's shaped like a heart. And it's so quiet and windless that it just fell. This balloon was probably sixty yards away from where I was standing, but it was so still and so quiet that when the balloon touched the ground, I heard it make a little crunch noise, even from that far away. It struck me as so serene, and there was some meaning to it that hit me so strongly.

It really felt as though the Universe was talking back to me that day after I'd talked to it the night before, and it seemed to be true because right after that, strange things started happening. My oldest daughter, who was also moving, suddenly found herself in a financial crunch and needed to borrow money from me, which took away from my moving fund, so I started looking for less expensive ways to move so that I could help her. I started noticing that some places had $99 move-in specials or first-month-free specials, so I went on craigslist and typed in "$99 move-ins" and lo and behold, this apartment in Tucson, Arizona, came up. I looked at the area it was in, and it looked pretty good on paper, so that's where I decided I was going to move.

So I got on a bus, and I chose to take a bus because I'd never taken one that far. Even though it was cheaper to take an airplane, I thought it would be an adventure, and it was. After two days, I finally made it to Tucson, and I got to my apartment complex and began my new life. I was really happy with my apartment, happy to be on my own, I was excited to see all the new plants and animals, excited about going out and taking pictures, so I started doing that, still not really having a direction in my life except that I felt that I was in the right place—I just didn't know why I was there. I was told a long time ago by my therapist that to find out what you want in life, you have to try things. So, not having a better plan, I decided to walk every street within my ability to walk. So I walked. It was nice being in a new place and seeing new things, but nothing felt profound to me at all, and being the non-exerciser I was at the time, I knew I wasn't going to last. I'm a realist about those things—I get bored quickly, and I knew I was go-ing to get bored quickly about this and probably quit walking, go back to my computer, start working, and live the same life I was living during my Year of Solitude, and then move on to Utah.

So on the last day I was going to walk, I found this other road that I hadn't known about. It looked like a good road to walk on, without a lot of traffic, and I decided to walk down that road as my last walk. And I'm taking pictures, and I see this tree that's very striking because it's basically dead—it has no leaves—but it's full of life—it has birds all over it—and as I'm taking pictures of that tree, I hear a voice behind me, and it says, "See anything interesting up there?"

I guess you have to know who I am to understand why I didn't look, I didn't make eye contact. I'd never felt that I was the kind of person that people would feel safe walking up to on a strange street to talk to me. When I finally did look, I saw this

beautiful woman who I really wouldn't have expected would find me approachable in the middle of a street, so right away I was intrigued because I never felt like a safe-looking person that a single woman would just walk up to and talk to like that. I immediately thought, "She must be here to sell me something," so I was on my guard. We walked and talked a little, and we immediately found that we had a lot in common, and she seemed genuinely interested in me, which I was surprised about. After the first quarter-mile or so of walking, she asked if I needed a walking buddy, and I said, "Heck, yeah," and I thought to myself, "Let's see where this path goes—maybe this is where my path is going," so I followed it. We became friends . . . and close friends . . . and lovers . . . and then she became my wife. She changed my life, and I hope I've changed hers.

We got married in April 2011. We had a tiny outdoor wedding with two friends and an officiant in a place with wild desert vegetation. As we were getting ready to set things up under a tree, a pyrrhuloxia—a close cousin of a cardinal—sat on a branch breathtakingly close to us for several moments and blessed the space.

Our vows:

From this day forward, I will treasure you as my companion, my equal, and my divine right partner. Loving what I know of you, trusting what I do not yet know, and having no illusions about who you are, I will respect your integrity and individuality. I will cherish and uplift you, be open with you, and bear witness to your life. I will revel and share in your joys and accomplishments, comfort you in times of sorrow, and be with you for all time.

I promise to be loyal and faithful, to celebrate the joys of life with you, and to give you my companionship and love. I promise to support your dreams and walk beside you, offering courage and strength in all your endeavors. I have faith in your abiding love for me and in all that life may bring us.

I vow to always strive for an intimacy that honors our bond while also allowing each of us to live a life as big as our capacities. I will continue to nurture our relationship as a sanctuary of warmth and peace, and a refuge of love and strength. As our intimacy deepens, I trust that the Universe will help us channel our love for the benefit of All That Is.

I feel incredibly fortunate to have found Charlie for countless reasons, among them the fact that his tribe—which is almost extinct; he's one of about ten left—was matriarchal, and there's not a shred of male supremacy in him. By the time we met, I was willing to be single for life rather than struggle with a partner over issues related to gender equality. It's a tremendous blessing to be in an intimate relationship completely free of that strife.

Another aspect of Charlie that contributes to our collective harmony is the fact that he did a lot of work in therapy before we met. He's remarkably emotionally literate and is as curious and welcoming of his emotions—and as committed to his growth and healing—as I am. He took to Internal Family Systems immediately and, like me, is clear on the importance of being a healing resource for himself rather than just relying on me for that. As our own first line of support, we're free to love each other without carrying each other. Our life together is filled with joy, affection, creativity, growth, playfulness, healthy boundaries, and respect for each other's needs and tender spots. When challenges arise, we work through them by speaking our truths, honoring our differences, trying on each other's perspective, deepening our compassion, finding helpful resources, seeking win/win solutions, and returning time and again to our deep love for each other.

～

My father's love for my mother was a great force guiding his life and opening doors to his growth and healing. Because his marriage sustained him so, he wanted each of his children to have a profoundly satisfying intimate relationship—what he called a "great love." His vision of me having a great love sustained my own dream, even through long years of despair and struggle. I once gave my father a simple plaque that said, "The greatest gift a father can give his children is to love their mother." He hung it over his workbench and reflected on it often. He was moved that I recognized the gift he was giving me by loving my mother so deeply. As a teenager, I was blind to this gift because I only saw him as the bad guy. As I matured and learned more about the complexity of human relationships, I grew to understand how he could love my mother and also have conflict with her, and I came to be comforted by the depth of his feelings for her.

At a gala celebration for my mother's seventieth birthday, guests were invited to reflect on her contribution to their lives. Friend after friend spoke about her with caring and respect. Then my father stood in front of the group. A Toastmasters graduate, he normally gave polished, humorous speeches. Tears welled in his eyes as he began to talk. "I was going to make a joke about the lumps in the oatmeal and such stuff, but I decided to play it straight this time. I want you to know, Bea, how deeply I love you and how much my world has grown and been enriched by being with you. Thank you for everything." I had tears in my eyes, too, and down my cheeks as well, feeling both his great love for her and his courage in sharing his feelings straightforwardly, not minimized or distracted by joking but instead pure and heartfelt.

As my relationship with Charlie continues to grow, I often reflect on this being the great love my father dreamed of for me as well as the one I dreamed of for myself. And I not only know this great love but am also blessed to have come to it with many relationship tools already in place that my parents either struggled for decades to develop or never found. Some of the hard work in their marriage helped clear a path for me. It's not always true that we repeat the patterns our parents model for us. Sometimes we learn from their hard times and build on their laborious progress. Sometimes we take the ball from them and run with it.

CHAPTER 19

Making Peace

A subtle yet steady transformation took place in my life during the years following my father's death. I began to notice that I was no longer consumed by the father issues I had struggled with in therapy. No longer did every man I encountered remind me of my father and set me off in some way.

What does it mean to say I've made peace with my father?

It doesn't mean that I've forgotten the past, that I pretend it didn't happen or disregard its effect on me. To do so would be to deny my history, to ignore the forces that have molded me into the person I am. Although I don't relish the pain of my past, I treasure the lessons I've learned—to speak my truths, to insist on being treated with humanity and respect, to develop my inner core to such an extent that I'm not shaken when someone challenges or disagrees with me. These are the fruits of the struggles, the rewards of being forced to grow strong enough to stand firm in the face of my father's criticism, threats, and violence. These are the lessons learned as I fought to hold on when the swirling waters around me tried to pull me loose from knowing and trusting myself.

When I was younger, I only knew how to let go and surrender to the current. Although I was aware of my inner core from an early age, I lost connection with it as the world around me intruded more and more. As I worked to grow stronger, I began to learn how *not* to surrender—how to resist the water's intentions for me.

In my delight at developing this new skill, I practiced it almost all the time, eventually discovering that I was building walls in the process of protecting myself. In recent years, I've been learning to navigate the currents, drawing on inner tools to determine when to swim hard and when to float on my back. Having a range of options gives me flexibility as well as a sense of directing my own life instead of living in reaction to others.

Making peace with my father means that my life is no longer circumscribed by what he did to me or how I was harmed by him. Healing from the past means no longer carrying our hard lessons as my cross to bear.

Healing also means being able to step outside my history enough to see how the world looked through my father's eyes. Learning about his past and the forces that shaped him has helped me understand his emotional pain and the challenges he faced in his life. This learning has equalized our relationship, allowing me to view him not only as my father but also as a fellow human being simply doing his best given the resources available to him.

In working through and releasing the struggles of my childhood, I often wanted my father to own up to what happened between us. Some of this desire came from a need to name the wounds and acknowledge dynamics that my family never spoke of. Naming these wounds broke a decades-old silence that preserved the myth of "one big, happy family." The myth left me no room to be honest, no space to acknowledge my pain, and therefore no way to heal and move on. Since that time I've learned a great deal about being authentic—with myself and with family members—and as a result I have grown.

Wanting my father to own up to the past was also rooted in a need for him to conform to my values and worldview. If only he could speak my language, if only he could provide the comfort to mend my pain with the magic words "I'm sorry I hurt you. Tell me what you need now in order to heal." Yet I came to understand that this, too, was part of my fantasy of the ideal father. And while occasionally I experience moments of grace when the perfect balm for my wounds appears, mostly I live in the gray area between all and nothing. I get something that helps, something new to work with, whether from a parent, teacher, therapist, friend, partner, or my own self blessing me with a new insight. I find ways to heal and move on—as an adult, though, not in a child's fantasyland where the entire world exists just to serve my needs.

I still struggle with the anxiety I carry in my cells, although it's much less paralyzing than it used to be. My personality has been stamped by a childhood of terror, and I suspect my healing will be a lifelong project. This is the legacy of abuse, and those who recommend just "giving it up" lack understanding of how people heal. Child abuse is profoundly damaging, and the terror it plants in a child persists, even with decades of hard work.

Yet the work of healing is now distinct from my father; I can acknowledge it as part of my life journey without hating my father for it. As an adult, it's my responsibility—not my father's or anyone else's—to nourish myself respectfully, to honor my tender and fiery nature and the unique gifts I carry, to embrace the continual unfolding of my life. When I was younger, I used to feel angry that it was my responsibility to do this, believing it was owed to me from outside. Now I feel freer precisely because it's within the scope of my control. Understanding that I'm the only person over whom I have any jurisdiction has allowed me to celebrate my autonomy and the freedom to live true to my own nature and dreams. It also has charged me with the responsibility of taking that autonomy seriously. If I don't care for myself well, no one else will do it for me.

~

I spent a good portion of my adult life raging against my dad for failing as a father. On and off for over twenty years, I worked on my father issues in therapy. That work helped me reclaim parts of myself that I'd lost touch with as a child due to my all-encompassing fear of him. The years in therapy, although grueling, were a crucial piece of the path to wholeness.

One day several months after my father's death, I found myself so filled with grief about losing him that I didn't know how I could go on. As I wept, I felt a distinct "click" in my body that was accompanied by a huge shift in my perception of him. He was no longer the angry, abusive father who did me wrong. He became instead a man who lived for seventy-four years, trying against difficult odds to keep alive his humor, his zest for life, his creativity, his delight in everyday joys; whose love for his wife constantly challenged him to grow beyond his limitations and fears; who fathered five children and did his best to teach us about integrity, principles, commitment. As I saw him in this new light, I began to see his life as a joyous success story, a testament to the love he carried within and the power of the love he drew to him. I could only feel immense gratitude to have been born to such a man.

His mother's oft-quoted line comes to mind: "If we wait long enough, everything will happen." If I had come to the fullness of this gratitude while he was still alive, I would have told him—but the healing between us was one of the gifts of his passing, and perhaps it never would have happened otherwise. At any rate, I'm sure that wherever he is, he knows.

For several years after my father's death, I kept seeing an image of my family as a circle, a band of people tied together by destiny, purpose, vision. Each time I saw this circle, I felt remorse that somehow we'd failed by losing him, by letting him slip through. I know now that the circle is unbroken, that he is still part of us, not only by existing in our memories and in the gifts he gave us, but also as a living presence who continues to nourish us. How I wish it could happen in the physical realm—how I long to sit and hold his hand for five minutes, make him a sandwich, or share a good joke—but he is still with us and we with him. Bonds this strong can't be severed by something as trivial as death.

My relationship with my father continues to grow. The deep lessons we moved through during his illness and death stay with me. I no longer hold him inside as a disapproving authority figure ready to lash out when I disobey him. Instead, I feel his unconditional love for me, his support of my path and my searchings. I no longer hear his voice telling me I'm making a mistake or teasing me because he doesn't know how else to deal with the ways in which I'm different from him. Instead I feel his faith and confidence in me. I hear him encouraging me to trust myself—to venture forth and live as fully as I can. And my motivations in life no longer come from a need to earn his approval any more than I feel compelled to rebel against him. My life is my own now, and I'm grateful for the figure of my father finally in its rightful place: no longer an unwelcome, critical intrusion in my mind but instead a loving presence who will always be with me.

APPENDIX A

Tools for Healing

The tools in this appendix are offered much like a platter of hors d'oeuvres to give you a taste of several kinds of inner work. They are not intended as a comprehensive treatment of each of the topics. The recommended reading in Appendix C includes resources for investigating these tools in greater depth.

If you are new to this kind of work, give yourself time to acclimate to the adventure of self-exploration. Some people take to it right away, while others learn to access their inner world more gradually. Like most everything in life, it gets easier with practice. Be gentle with yourself and honor your own pace.

The tools included in this section—active imagination, art, journaling, and working with the observer self and subpersonalities—are rich ways to work with the unconscious, a part of our mind that contains material of which we are mostly unaware in everyday life. In the words of Jungian analyst Robert A. Johnson,

The unconscious is a marvelous universe of unseen energies, forces, forms of intelligence—even distinct personalities—that live within us. It is a much larger realm than most of us realize, one that has a complete life of its own running parallel to the ordinary life we live day to day. The unconscious is the secret source of much of our thought, feeling, and behavior. It influences us in ways that are all the more powerful because unsuspected. (Inner Work, p. 3)

While the unconscious is by definition not conscious, the parts closest to consciousness and most ready to come into awareness can be accessed and engaged with a good dose of intention and the assistance of various tools. I think of this process as the leading edge of our individual healing.

The native language of the unconscious is the language of symbols. By accessing these symbols and bringing them to consciousness, we can work with their energies and develop a relationship with them. Working with our inner symbols can strengthen the connection between conscious and unconscious aspects of self, providing for increasingly open communication between the two as well as strengthening intuitive abilities.

You might have an intuition to talk with an imaginary giant orange parrot, to draw a secret underground world, to write a letter to a grandparent you never met, or to acknowledge a needy child part of yourself. The trick is to follow through on the intuition without first trying to make sense of it—in other words, to trust that the intuition is worth exploring without first filtering it through the rational mind.

The tools in this appendix can facilitate the expression of intuitive promptings in safe ways and in a safe setting. This doesn't mean you'll go out into the world in an uncensored way; it means you'll learn how to explore deeper levels of yourself in private. This work can help you integrate unconscious, or shadow, aspects of yourself that you may currently be expressing in ways that do not serve your well-being (such as addictions, dysfunctional relationships, self-sabotage, illness, and more). This work can also contribute to global healing, as is eloquently expressed in this quote by Deborah Daw Heffernan:

I have always believed that each and every one of us is respon-
sible for doing her own emotional homework, for doing the best
we can with our gifts and constraints. The process of facing down
our ghosts is our small, attainable contribution to a kinetic pro-
cess that holds the potential for healing the world. And why not?
After all, the opposite is true: history has proven that people who
are unwilling to catch and release their individual sadnesses,
disappointments, and hidden motivations have compensated by
wreaking havoc on the world. Good and evil lie within each of
us, and every day we choose which potential to fill.

(*An Arrow Through the Heart*, p. 190)

Active Imagination

In the book *Inner Work*, Robert Johnson delineates two ways
of working with symbols in the unconscious—active imagination
and dreamwork. Active imagination accesses these symbols in a
waking state, while dreamwork accesses them during sleep. (I do
not include dreamwork in this appendix because I lack sufficient
background to present the topic. However, dreamwork can be a
rich tool for doing inner work, and many books, including Johnson's, exist for those interested in working with their dreams.)

Active imagination, a process developed by Carl Jung, refers
to various means of exploring unconscious material through the
use of creative fantasy, giving voice to images and symbols in the
unconscious. Active imagination involves bringing the images to
consciousness and engaging with them through the use of dialogue. The dialogue can be spoken, written, drawn, danced, or
anything else you can think of. (I focus on spoken and written
dialogue in this section; see the section on art therapy for a discussion of art and other nonverbal modes of expression.) The "Conversations with My Father" chapter of this book is an example of
dialogues that were spoken aloud, recorded, and later transcribed.

I have also conversed with images in complete silence. There are no rules—it's about discovering what works best for you and takes you to a place where you can effectively engage with the images and discover their messages.

A good skill to cultivate in doing active imagination and other inner work is the ability to do what I call "catching the tail" of buried thoughts and feelings by noticing and allowing into awareness the first thing that comes to your mind. "Catching the tail" helps bring forth symbols hovering on the fence between unconsciousness and consciousness. To develop the skill of "catching the tail," pay attention to whatever comes into your awareness if someone asks what you're feeling or what your preference is in a given situation. If your first instinct is to deny the feeling or quash the impulse to voice your own desires, it's a clue that the "tail" you're trying to catch is buried. Affirm your wish to become aware of your feelings and desires, and keep practicing. Welcoming your authentic responses makes more space for them in your life.

Active imagination isn't simply a mental exercise—it's also an energetic and emotional engagement with our images and symbols. In Johnson's words:

> *This experience, to be sure, is symbolic. The images with whom we interact are symbols, and we encounter them on a symbolic plane of existence. But a magical principle is at work: When we experience the images, we also directly experience the inner parts of ourselves that are clothed in the images. This is the power of symbolic experience in the human psyche when it is entered into consciously: Its intensity and its effect on us is often as concrete as a physical experience would be. Its power to realign our attitudes, teach us and change us at deep levels, is much greater than that of external events that we may pass through without noticing.* (*Inner Work*, p. 25)

Johnson provides a note of caution, repeated here, to people new to active imagination. It's important to have access to someone who can help you in the event that you feel overwhelmed by the imagination or can't cut it off when you want to. To newcomers, the images may at times feel powerful enough to overtake your personality, and the emotions you access may feel too strong or vivid. Be sure you have someone to call on for help and grounding as needed until you become familiar with the process.

Feeling overwhelmed is rarely a problem, however, and in fact the opposite is generally true—people often have more difficulty immersing themselves in their imagination than separating themselves from it. However, until you know how you will respond, it's best to have a safety net.

Keep in mind that opening a door to your inner world rarely happens in one sitting. If you're accustomed to pushing away that world in your everyday life, it's not going to magically appear full-blown the first time you open the door. Much like a person who's been dismissed repeatedly, your inner awareness is likely to doubt your sincerity the first few times you invite it to reveal itself. Demonstrate your good intentions by extending the invitation repeatedly instead of giving up if you don't have a cosmic experience the first time.

You can also demonstrate your good intentions by being willing to take what comes. You might hope for a fairy godmother dressed in powder blue and a halo who will offer you clear, loving, and inspired guidance. If you instead get a giant alligator with razor-sharp teeth and wicked-looking eyes (as once happened to me), try to stay with the process and hear what it has to say. And remember that you get to have a voice, too. If you're afraid of the alligator, tell it. If you want it to move back twenty feet, say so and then make it happen. Find a balance between honoring your need for safety and your desire to step outside your comfort zone in order to cultivate a relationship with your unconscious. If the alligator showed up, you can trust that something rich and valuable can emerge from dialoguing with it.

Try This: Invite Images Through Active Imagination

• Find a quiet space and time away from your everyday routine. Arrange to be free of interruption by family members, pets, and the telephone. Set an intention to engage in an active imagination exercise.

• Sit with pen and paper, or at a computer, and invite a voice, image, or energy from your unconscious to make itself known. Wait to see what wants to emerge. Open yourself to whatever is there, and remember to "catch the tail" of any fleeting words, thoughts, or impressions that pop into your mind.

• If an image appears, whether familiar or unfamiliar, begin a dialogue by simply asking, "Who are you? Why have you come to me?" Then engage in conversation in whatever way feels appropriate. Depending on what appears—say, that giant orange parrot—it might not feel "appropriate" at all and may in fact feel bizarrely unfamiliar. Give yourself the freedom to get curious and explore without imposing conventional constraints on the experience. Remember, this is your imagination at work. Don't worry about what the neighbors will think; they'll never know unless you choose to tell them.

• If no image appears, keep in mind that this state of pure receptivity does not come naturally to many people. If this is the case, try one of the techniques below to facilitate the process. The techniques are deliberate methods for beginning the process, but remember that once begun, you'll need to let go of the reins and allow things to unfold organically. Active imagination doesn't work if you impose a map on it; it only works if you allow images and information to emerge freely from your unconscious (though you're free to stop it at any time).

— Choose an image from a recurring fantasy, such as an idealized child or lover, or an animal that captivates your attention. You can also choose a person who has died with whom you wish to connect, as I did in the "Conversations with My Father" chapter.

— Choose a figure that has appeared in a dream, perhaps one that you found particularly intriguing or offensive. Either way, the figure clearly carries a lot of energy for you. Hold the intent to reenter the dream and see what wants to happen next.

— Go to a safe place in your imagination, perhaps a beach, forest, private garden, or special room. Wait there for an image to appear.

— Identify a feeling or mood, and ask for an image to appear of who is feeling that way. (This is discussed further in the Subpersonalities section of this appendix.)

• Once you have an image to work with, allow a dialogue to unfold by letting your imagination lead the way. Ask the image why it has come to you and what it wants you to know. Adopt a welcoming stance as much as possible, letting the image know you're willing to listen to what it has to say. Feel free to say no to any activity that feels wrong to you, but as much as possible, discuss with the image why you don't want to participate. Include your feelings as well as your thoughts in the dialogue.

• As the dialogue unfolds, write down everything that happens and every verbal exchange. In addition to being able to refer to it later, keeping a written record helps you stay focused on the process and can prevent your mind from wandering. If you take to the process naturally and find that you stay focused with ease, you may prefer to speak and record everything that happens and transcribe the tape later.

• The dialogue is a give-and-take between your conscious self and your unconscious. While it's important to allow images to express themselves, it's unwise to give them free rein to run your life. If, for example, an image asks you to abandon all your responsibilities, you must bring your values to bear on your response. Again, you can and should say no to anything that feels wrong to you, but be sure to use this opportunity to get to know the part of you that wants to abandon all responsibilities. If it lives in your unconscious, it's probably already been impacting some aspect of your life, possibly through sabotage. By developing a relationship with it, you'll make it more conscious and find ways to balance its desires with the rest of you. (This topic is discussed in greater depth in the Observer Self and Subpersonalities sections of this appendix.)

• Ideally, it's best to stay with the image until a resolution takes place. The image emerged from your unconscious, and there's a reason it did. It wants to help you see or understand something that represents a next step in your growth. If you can't stay with the image because the experience is too intense, make an agreement to revisit the image after you've had time to assimilate what has happened. The process might require a series of active imagination sessions to resolve. In some cases, you might develop a relationship with an image over the course of months or even years.

• When a resolution has taken place and your active imagination experience is complete, create a concrete expression of it. This might be a ritual, a drawing or collage, or whatever feels appropriate—but definitely something that involves your emotions and your body. This activity will ground the experience in your cells and connect the symbols in your unconscious with your everyday life, which will facilitate integration of the experience.

The Observer Self

As discussed earlier, the observer self is an aspect of the psyche that can step back from everyday life and observe from a larger vantage point. You might consider it your inner wisdom or a wise aspect of yourself that you're able to access in calm, clear moments. Your observer self is connected to your core self, which can be likened to the hub of the wheel of your personality. While your moods and behaviors vary, the observer self operates from a perspective that can help to make sense of it all, and even more, can help you integrate these diverse aspects. The observer self is an invaluable ally in personal growth and healing that you can "turn up the volume" on over time.

Try This: Contact Your Observer Self

- Find a quiet space and time away from your everyday routine. Arrange to be free of interruption by family members, pets, and the telephone.

- Close your eyes and take several deep breaths to calm yourself. Notice the feeling of the breath as it enters your body and fills you, and again as it leaves your body. Repeat this several times as you continue to notice the sensations that accompany your breathing.

- Notice any other sensations you may feel in your body—tension, relaxation, comfort or discomfort, hot or cold. Don't try to change the sensations; simply notice them.

- Direct your attention to any sounds you may hear around you— birds singing, the refrigerator humming, traffic whooshing by outside. Whatever you hear, just notice it. Notice how directing your attention to the outside sounds diminishes your awareness of the sensations in your body. Notice that you can shift your focus back and forth between internal sensations and external sounds.

• Now direct your attention to your feelings. Notice how you're feeling in this moment—happy, sad, angry, calm, agitated, or another emotion. Again, don't try to change the feelings; simply notice them. Notice also that when you tune in to your emotions, your awareness of sounds diminishes.

• Next, direct your attention to your thoughts. Notice the thoughts that are present in your awareness when you ask yourself, "What am I thinking right now?" Again, just notice what's there without trying to change anything.

• Review briefly your experience of directing your awareness, in turn, to your breath, other body sensations, the sounds in your environment, your feelings, and your thoughts. Imagine your attention as a spotlight you can aim at will in any of these directions. Review once again the places where you directed your awareness as you imagine shining a spotlight on each of them.

• Now ask yourself, "Who is aware? Who is this being who directs awareness? Who is this being who is outside of, yet aware of, all these experiences?"

This is your observer self, who is capable of identifying with or disidentifying from any experience you're having. When you have access to your observer self, you can strengthen the ability to step outside of any mood, feeling, or urge that surfaces and discover a greater power to direct your life instead of being at the effect of impulses that seem to overtake you. Your observer self can also help you learn about those impulses and listen with compassion and clarity to their wisdom and the messages they have for you. (The observer self is discussed further in the next section.)

Subpersonalities

A key concept I touch on throughout this book is that of sub-personalities (also called parts, aspects, ego states, and fragments in the psychological literature). Subpersonalities are aspects within each of us that have their own distinct thoughts and feelings. Some subpersonalities can be considered different "hats" we wear in various aspects of our lives: as spouse, parent, employee, or hobbyist. More extreme subpersonalities may have been created as a result of wounding (including, but not limited to, abuse and other trauma) and sometimes hold thoughts and emotions that "go underground," splitting off from the core of our personality because staying connected to them during painful moments was too difficult. It is not necessary to have a history of abuse or other trauma to benefit from working with these parts of us.

Subpersonalities are normal aspects of all of us, although the internal cast of characters varies from person to person. We may have aspects that embody the intellectual, taskmaster, adventurer, magical child, hermit, lover, competitor, topdog, underdog, and so on. Some subpersonalities are archetypal; that is, they embody blueprints of universal energies. Other subpersonalities are idealized images of oneself, such as Brad Pitt, Jennifer Lopez, Don Juan, or Mother Teresa. These idealized subpersonalities often appear in adolescence as young people try on various adult energies. Still other subpersonalities represent specific functions or aspects of self, such as thinking, feeling, and self-protection.

For various reasons, each of us has certain aspects that become unconscious, or "go underground." They can sabotage growth and can also wreak havoc on our lives. Like a child who wants attention but is repeatedly ignored or turned away, disowned subpersonalities can grow increasingly insistent on being heard and may have unique ways of throwing temper tantrums. For example, a healthy need for a break from responsibilities, if denied, can manifest in a serious illness that mandates rest or an impulsive trip right before a critical work deadline. An ignored subpersonality can also spark rage attacks and even outbursts of violence.

Disowned subpersonalities may seem to disappear completely, when in reality they are dormant or in hiding. This kind of disconnection from a subpersonality tends to limit a person's life in some way. For example, a healthy need for emotional expression, if denied, can develop over time into a complete lack of authentic emotion or, in some cases, contempt for authentic emotion. A healthy need for sexual expression, if denied, can cause myriad forms of internal disconnection that can range from completely rejecting the body to becoming a sexual abuser. This is seen in religious zealots who preach abstinence while acting out as pedophiles.

Identifying our subpersonalities and developing relationships with them can be a rich way to expand self-awareness; decode seemingly weird impulses, behaviors, and symptoms; and bring us into greater alignment with our core self. Over time, we can learn what triggers each of them and what needs each one is trying to express. We can learn to welcome them as helpful reminders of the need to slow down, find our voice, heal a past trauma, bring more beauty into our life, integrate a hidden need, or respond to other messages they may carry.

As you explore your subpersonalities, keep in mind that you're in charge. Neglected subpersonalities can get stubborn and militant if they've been ignored for a long time. It's important to listen to their essential message, but you are the final authority—they don't get to run the show. And the more you develop relationships with them over time, the less they will run the show.

(See the Internal Family Systems listings in Appendix C for additional resources for working with subpersonalities.)

Try This: Discover Your Subpersonalities
(Adapted with permission from *What We May Be*, by Piero Ferrucci, pp. 48–49)

• Find a quiet space and time away from your everyday routine. Arrange to be free of interruption for this exercise.

• Reflect on a prominent trait, quality, or attitude of yours. You might choose the first one that comes to mind.

• Close your eyes and focus your attention on this aspect of yourself. Allow an image to spontaneously emerge that represents this aspect of you. It could be a human form (adult or child), an animal, a plant, a make-believe being, a rock, a car, or anything else in the entire world. Don't intentionally choose an image; rather, allow an image to reveal itself to you. Whatever comes is the right thing.

• When the image appears, be aware of it without interference or judgment. If interference or judgment is present to such a degree that you can't separate from it, make that the focus of this exercise.

• If the image changes or moves as you focus on it, just continue to observe it and allow it to show itself to you. Then become aware of the general feeling or energy of the image.

• Allow the image to communicate with you in whatever way it wishes. Regardless of whether it appears as animate or inanimate, it can communicate. Ask what it needs and what it wants you to know, and simply give it space to answer. This image you are observing and listening to is a subpersonality. It has a life of its own—its own feelings, needs, and motives.

- Open your eyes and write down everything that has taken place during this exercise. When you have finished, give the subpersonality any name that will help you remember and identify it later on, such as Nicey Nice, the Bully, Igor the Monster, Gimme, the Cynic, the Whiner, and so on. After you've named it, record everything you know about its personality, traits, preferences, and anything else it has shared with you. Take as much time as you need to learn all you can about this subpersonality.

- When you are finished, or at a different time, revisit this subpersonality to see if there's more to learn from it.

- At a different time, get acquainted with a different subpersonality by repeating the steps above. If you wish, you can again reflect on a prominent trait, quality, or attitude you hold. Another method for identifying a subpersonality is to recall a time when you behaved in a way that you consider atypical. Perhaps you later said something like, "I just wasn't myself" or "I don't know what came over me. That's not at all like me." Who was that? Give it room to step forward into your awareness and gently begin to get acquainted with it.

Try This: Work with Your Subpersonalities
- *Identification/Disidentification*—Choose one of your subpersonalities (I'll use Nicey Nice as an example) and recall a time when it seemed to be "running the show." Remember how it feels to be filled with Nicey Nice's energy. Feel that energy in your body. Walk around the room as Nicey Nice. Give yourself some lines as if you're playing a part in a movie, such as "Whatever you want is fine with me" or "I'm not angry. I don't believe in being angry." Now shake off that energy and step back into the role of your observer self. Reflect on the fact that sometimes the energy of that subpersonality overtakes you. Reflect on the

fact that you can step outside of it. Write about what you just experienced.

- *Observer Self Conversation/Dialogue*—Have a conversation between your observer self and a subpersonality, either aloud or as a written dialogue. If you notice the conversation becoming tense or heated, explore the possibility that a second subpersonality joined the conversation. You can expand the conversation to include this new subpersonality.

- *Conversations Between Subpersonalities*—Choose two of your subpersonalities who seem to have something to say to each other. You might choose two who are at odds with each other or two who could become allies. Allow them to dialogue. Notice the different emotions and bodily sensations when each one is speaking. Write about your experience.

- *Reluctant Subpersonalities*—If you encounter a hint of a subpersonality that is reluctant to talk or otherwise engage with you, give it the space it needs. If it's been neglected for a long time, it might not trust your intentions or might feel confronted and unsafe. The first step in getting to know it is simply being aware of it. The next step is to allow it to be however it is without trying to change it. Over time, as it sees that you're not going to attack it or force it to go away or change, it might decide to open up.

- *Obstinate Subpersonalities*—Explore the possibility of negotiating with an obstinate or otherwise difficult subpersonality. Each one is expressing a valid, even if distorted, need or concern. Try taking a step in the subpersonality's direction, and ask it, in turn, to take a step in your direction. Over time, an initial compromise can lead to further common ground.

Art Therapy

Art therapy is a powerful tool for engaging with the unconscious and bringing aspects of self into awareness. As discussed earlier, art therapy has nothing to do with artistic talent—it's simply a way to give voice to inner symbols. You may feel an impulse to create literal representations of people, houses, and other things in your life. Or you might draw energetic, symbolic, or scribbly representations of those things—or even images whose meanings elude you completely. Release the notion that either literal or symbolic is the "right" way to draw. Trust that the perfect images that "want out" will emerge; get out of the way and allow your inner self to express itself. Give yourself time to develop fluency with this medium of expression. Much like learning a foreign language, getting comfortable with accessing inner symbols may take time.

In order to give yourself to the art process, it's important to let go of ideas or plans about what you want to create or what it might mean. The goal of this work is listening and responding to impulses and intuitions using art materials. You might also have some cognitive understanding of what the artwork means. If you do, that's fine, but you can trust that even without the understanding, you're giving voice to a part of yourself by honoring your inner impulses. Over a period of weeks, months, or years, you might see themes develop.

Try This: Explore with Art

- Find a quiet space and time away from your everyday routine. Arrange to be free of interruption by family members, pets, and the telephone. Put on some mellow instrumental music or simply enjoy the silence.

- Sit with whatever art materials you feel prompted to use (see Materials discussion at the end of this section). I'll use drawing paper and oil pastels as an example for this exercise.

- Close your eyes and take several slow breaths, mentally releasing any thoughts you might have. Imagine for this period of time that your concerns have evaporated, and give yourself the gift of this time for yourself. As much as possible, also release ideas, plans, and expectations.

- Affirm your intention to listen to and honor whatever wisdom wants to emerge from your inner self. Be open to something completely unexpected showing up.

- If you feel so inclined, place your hands palms down on the paper, close your eyes, and ask the question, "What wants to emerge right now?" You may see an image in your mind, hear a word or phrase, or get a sensation of something that wants attention. If so, feel free to express it on paper or in another way that feels right to you. For example, if you feel an impulse to crumple a piece of paper and throw it at a wall, do it!

- If you don't receive an impression, ask yourself these questions and follow up with whatever action feels like the most immediate response to each question.
    — What color does my hand want to pick up?
    — What movement does my hand want to make?
    — What color next?
    — What wants to emerge?
    Allow yourself to get into a flow of attuning to the intuitive impulses you're feeling. Notice how "in the present" you feel when you attune in this way and how the rest of your life seems to drop away. This quality of presence is deeply nourishing. It's a natural stress reducer, and it's also a great way to bypass your inner critic or censor.

- Follow your impulses to create whatever image wants to come out. Take your time and continue to check in with yourself. Sense when the image is complete. There's no need to think about whether the page is filled. Empty spaces can be part of the process, too.

• If a part of your drawing feels particularly intriguing, surprising, or disturbing, you may want to try a technique called magnifying to explore it further. Use a new piece of paper to enlarge that section of your drawing, filling in details and other elements in whatever way your intuition prompts you. You may want to continue magnifying over a number of drawings or revisit the process over a series of days.

• If you have a sense of the meaning of your artwork, journaling can be a useful tool for exploring and recording the insights that come to you. If you don't have a sense of the meaning, you can still journal about how the experience felt, or try freewriting (see the section on Journaling). Even without knowing what your art "means," you still may notice that you felt nourished by the process. Perhaps it was the quiet time for yourself, or maybe it was the experience of expressing yourself with color and shapes instead of words. The images you drew might be part of a bigger process—perhaps a part of you needing attention that will emerge in greater fullness over time.

• If you are working with issues related to the body (embodiment, health, and so on), you might find it fruitful to get a large piece of butcher paper and have someone trace the outline of your body. Cut the paper long enough to leave extra room above and below your body in case you want to surround your body with colors, shapes, or words. Sit with the tracing until it speaks to you; then use art materials to fill in and/or surround the outline as you feel prompted. Take time to journal afterward.

• Remember that your art is for you; it's not for anyone else's eyes unless you want to share it. If you do, I recommend explaining beforehand that you prefer the other person to simply witness silently—to look at your art and listen to your experience with sensitivity. Because your images come from a deep place inside, other people's associations often aren't appropriate or useful.

Materials

You might enjoy experimenting with various media. Oil pastels (similar to crayons but with denser color) are among the easiest and cleanest to use. I sometimes use oil pastels for small drawings before bedtime because they're simple to use and clean up after. Chalk pastels are messier because they create chalk dust (a plastic tablecloth is recommended if you don't have an art room); however, their color is more easily blended and can be applied in many ways. I'm especially fond of applying them to my fingers and finger painting with them. I like the soft, subtle color blending I can achieve and the soft way I feel inside when I caress the colors. I also enjoy using chalk pastels to express passionate feelings, which are magnified by the vibrant colors and flying chalk dust.

You may want to experiment with other media, including clay, various kinds of paint (including face paint), mask making, and collage (including three-dimensional collage using a glue gun and found objects). You can also experiment with various kinds of paper. You may find that certain materials are best for particular moods. When I feel a need to release anger, I like black and red oil pastels on eighteen by twenty-four newsprint. When I feel an impulse to explore a kind of energy, such as the feminine, I often create a collage with magazine images (*National Geographic* is one of my favorites). When I feel restless and want to explore where I'm going—figuratively or literally—I often make a collage using a map as the base paper. Various materials offer different experiences of body involvement as well. If you feel prompted to involve your entire body, try a big chunk of clay or do some finger painting on a large piece of butcher paper.

Other Expressive Therapies

Art therapy falls under the umbrella of expressive arts therapies. This field also includes music therapy, dance/movement therapy, drama therapy, and more. If you feel drawn to these kinds of inner work, many resources exist for learning about them, including books, workshops, websites, and professional trainings.

Journaling

Journaling, like art, is a tool for accessing more of ourselves than we're consciously aware of in everyday life. It's a way to connect with the life energy that flows through each of us—the deeper person we each are at our core—as well as our many subpersonalities. Like art, journaling is an intentional act that over time strengthens our connection to our inner world. It's a way to get to know who we are beneath our conditioning—to step outside of the person we present to the world. Some people experience art or movement as their native language and use words as a secondary language. Others who feel more naturally connected to words may be particularly fond of journaling.

The more your everyday life speeds up from deadlines, crises, a drive to overachieve, or the frenzied pace of the modern world, the more you may find your intuitive side yearning for balance in the form of stillness. Journaling can be a way to find that stillness.

Journaling can be about discovering the place inside where feelings, choices, impulses, and motivations come from. It's a way to express inner aspects of your life, which over time may come together like a connect-the-dots exercise. Things get clearer as threads and themes emerge that have been percolating underground. This, in turn, can allow you to live a more conscious, intentional life and to reframe your outlook from a deeper perspective.

Some of the power of journaling is in the act of naming. You may feel in your body a sense of relief and resonance—an "aha"—

when you've found the right words to describe a feeling or experience. You may know how affirming it feels to be deeply heard and understood by another person; journaling allows you to do that for yourself—to be your own best confidante. It's an act of self-witnessing, a way to affirm that your life is worthy of attention and respect. In truth, no one else has the capacity to love and honor you as fully as you can love and honor yourself because only you know what you truly need. And paradoxically, only by learning to love and honor yourself can you know that experience enough to fully receive it from others.

A journal can take the form of a blank book, a spiral-bound notebook, a computer, a roll of butcher paper, or anything else that feels right to you. You may even choose to speak into a tape recorder and transcribe your words later. Choosing the right journal and writing implement can be a creative act, a way of expressing your intention to honor your own tastes and desires. Some people enjoy using an artist's sketchbook and combining writing with art; portable art supplies such as colored pencils or a twelve-pack of oil pastels can be welcome adjuncts to the right pen or pencil.

Where and when you write are as personal as what you use to write. Journaling in the morning or before bedtime, at a neighborhood cafe, with your back against a tree, or in a different place on different days—it's completely up to you. Many people find it works best to be away from their daily routine and be free of family members, dirty dishes, and the perennial to-do list. Others only feel safe enough to delve into their deepest thoughts and feelings in the comfort of familiar, enclosed surroundings. There are no rules save one: do what feels right.

As with art, it's good to practice suspending judgment and asking your inner critic or censor to take a break. The more you can do this, the freer your inner self will feel to let out whatever wants out. You can go back later and extract meaning or, as with art, just let it cook and deliver insights in its own time.

Try This: Explore with Journaling

- *Freewrite*—Ask yourself a question, such as "What is my sadness/anger/fear about?" or "How do I feel about what just happened with my mother?" Then start writing and keep writing, nonstop, in a stream-of-consciousness style. Your writing will take you to places you didn't expect, and you're likely to learn some very interesting things about yourself.

- *Write with a Timer*—Set a timer for five or ten minutes and freewrite nonstop. If you run out of words, write your last sentence over again and again or write your first sentence again. Write what it's like for you when your mind is blank. Or if your mind is wandering, check out where it's leading you. Keep writing.

- *Start with a Phrase*—Choose a phrase, such as "I never knew," as a starting point for journaling. Write twenty sentences that start with the phrase. Here are a few of mine:
    — I never knew that I found myself when I was nine.
    — I never knew I had a penchant for anger.
    — I never knew that all good things are lost.
    — I never knew that before the rain, you can smell it coming.
    Other possible starting phrases include: I feel, I need, I hope, I believe, I fear, I love, I hate, I mourn, I am, I won't, and I will. Or make up your own based on what's inside that wants out.

- *Make a List*—One hundred things you're angry about, scared of, frustrated with, yearning for. One hundred wishes you have for your life. One hundred qualities you want to bring into your life. If you run out of things before you reach one hundred, ask yourself repeatedly, "And what else?" One hundred of anything will likely get to the heart of your thoughts and feelings.

- *Write a Letter to Someone Else*—As a journaling exercise, write a letter to someone who is deceased or someone with whom you have unfinished business (a parent, child, sibling, ex-partner, boss, and so on). Affirm before starting to write that you're under no obligation to share the letter with anyone; this exercise is specifically for giving voice to your feelings and thoughts. It's completely up to you whether you choose later to act on what you wrote in some way—there's no right or wrong.

- *Write a Letter to Yourself from Someone Else*—Write a letter to yourself from someone who is deceased or someone with whom you have unfinished business. Just see what comes.

- *Dialogue with Your Body or a Body Part*—This can be particularly fruitful if you are experiencing a physical challenge. Your body, or a particular part of your body, might hold some wisdom that you're ready to hear.

- *Write a Letter to Your Inner Critic*—If you have a particularly loud inner critic, write a letter to it or dialogue with it. When you have finished, reflect on where that critical voice came from.

- *Collect Quotations That Inspire You*—Collect quotations on any topic you'd like to think about more—grieving, living an authentic life, finding soul sustenance in nature, writers on writing—whatever feels right to you. Use the quotations as jumping-off points for freewriting.

- *Write for Ritual Release*—Write on a piece of paper something you're ready to release from your life—perhaps an old relationship, a bad habit, or a belief that no longer serves you. Place several large stones in the bottom of a Pyrex bowl, put the paper in the bowl, and set the paper on fire. As it burns, feel in your body the energy of that person, quality, or thing leaving your life. Feel the space that is now available for new possibilities.

Your unconscious is a rich world with unlimited resources for exploration, healing, and adventure. Nurturing a relationship with this part of you can reawaken natural knowing and support the development of a full, authentic life. It can also reveal a wellspring of wisdom and strength to help during times of difficulty and loss. May the tools in this appendix be as useful to you as they have been to me.

Psychological Concepts

A brief discussion of several psychological concepts is presented here as context for understanding certain aspects of my story. Alice Miller, the respected Swiss psychologist, has written widely on the topic of child abuse, including *The Drama of the Gifted Child* and *For Your Own Good: Hidden Cruelty in Child-Rearing and the Roots of Violence*. Miller's books are useful for anyone seeking to learn more about the origins and consequences of child abuse. Her writings have helped me make sense of my difficult childhood.

Miller's basic premise is that severe psychological damage results when children are raised by people who use humiliation, violence, and excessive force. Discipline that demands rigid obedience and the suppression of anger, sadness, and fear—healthy emotions and natural responses to life's challenges—forces children to repress, or "put away," those parts of themselves that their caretakers punish. Instead of being eliminated, however, those put-away parts go underground and become "split off."

I discussed the concept of subpersonalities in Appendix A. My clinical experience leads me to believe that the formation of subpersonalities during trauma creates polar-opposite qualities in a child's personality. One quality becomes an exaggerated personality trait, while its opposite is often relegated to unconsciousness or covert expression. Because abused children are victimized by authority figures who use power inappropriately, they commonly develop split-off subpersonalities related to issues of power and authority. I developed an ultra-compliant subpersonality who avoided making waves or calling attention to myself in order to escape being targeted by my father's rage. Its polar opposite was my "inner rebel," who harbored hidden rage and staged elaborate mutinies in my imagination, which I acted out by stealing and compulsively overeating.

This kind of splitting accounts for the behavior of people who commit acts of extreme violence but are described by neighbors or schoolmates as people who'd "never hurt a fly." The more extreme a person's good-girl or nice-guy surface appearance, the more likely the presence of a flip side in his or her unconscious. Fortunately, the flip sides of most people are rarely extreme enough to express in acts of drastic violence, such as "going postal" or slaughtering classmates. But these flip sides often show up in less extreme, yet still highly problematic, ways such as shaming or bullying children or covert forms of control, or in flattened emotions due to habitually and unconsciously suppressing one's vitality. They may also manifest in addictions and illness.

Subpersonalities formed by trauma have the capacity to operate outside our volition. We've all engaged in behaviors we consider atypical that are triggered by a comment or an event. "I don't know who that was," we might say, "I just wasn't myself." Unless we work purposefully to heal these subpersonalities, they continue to operate semi-autonomously—and sometimes completely autonomously, as in the case of people with dissociative identity disorder (formerly called multiple personality disorder). If there is a history of trauma or abuse, subpersonalities work is best done with the assistance of a skilled licensed psychotherapist.

Even with purposeful healing work, subpersonalities don't disappear altogether; instead, they continue to exist as semi-distinct aspects of personality with which we can develop healthy relationships. Subpersonalities can often then be respected as expressions of our various needs. For example, when my inner rebel becomes activated, it often serves as a signal that I'm feeling powerless or that I'm in the presence of someone who uses power inappropriately. That awareness allows me to respond by choosing whether to handle the situation assertively, remove myself from the person's presence, or comfort myself when faced with true powerlessness, as in the loss of my father.

Subpersonalities may continue to hold memories of the conditions under which they were formed. Time often collapses when subpersonalities are activated such that events from decades ago may be experienced as though they're happening right now. Several of my subpersonalities, still in the grip of vivid memories of my father's rage, weren't convinced that the violence had ended until my father was comatose and near death, even though the physical abuse had stopped more than twenty years earlier.

Working to heal subpersonalities formed by trauma can be achieved by accessing an aspect of ourselves called the observer self, the adult observer, or, in Internal Family Systems therapy, the Self. This aspect of the psyche allows us to recenter ourselves by disidentifying with, and developing a conscious relationship with, our various subpersonalities. The observer self may be thought of as our inner wisdom, our soul, or an internal core of compassion, clarity, and calm. The observer self can engage in or oversee dialogues with wounded subpersonalities and help establish more trusting and integrated relationships with and between them. The observer self can also help create more balance in our everyday life. Over time, we can develop a sense that our observer self—rather than various wounded subpersonalities—is in charge. As we continue to exercise this muscle, we create a positive feedback loop.

Getting acquainted with and healing split-off subpersonalities may involve accessing painful, even traumatic, childhood memories. Anger may be an initial response as these memories return to consciousness. Opening to this awareness means acknowledging that our parents made terrible mistakes, whether or not intentional. *This is not about blame—it's about better understanding the forces that have shaped our emotions and behaviors.* Over time, the anger may transform into grief about what we needed but didn't receive as a child, often accompanied by a deep sense of compassion for the child-self who suffered. As this compassion grows, it may also allow for compassion toward our parents, who doubtless also suffered as children and whose parenting was shaped by that suffering.

Developing the ability to disidentify with and relate consciously to wounded subpersonalities is useful in reclaiming sovereignty over our life. Equally important is the ability to learn to feel authentic emotions. Abused children often cut off, or dissociate, from their emotions while the abuse is occurring. This survival strategy—an appropriate defense that shields children from the worst of their terror—often becomes an automatic reaction persisting into adulthood that restricts access to emotions. Some survivors lack access to particular emotions, such as anger or sadness, while others may be emotionally muted in general or may only have access to either happy or unhappy feelings.

Just as the body has intrinsic ways of mending a laceration or broken bone, so the psyche has emotions as its mechanism for psychological healing. We need only watch a young child bruised in a playground fall to see the initial outpouring of tears and agitation, which, if allowed to proceed unimpeded, eventually releases, followed by a return to calm. In this way, emotions allow us to process daily life in much the same way as cleaning a fish tank, removing old debris (hurts and traumas) and returning the water to clarity. In contrast, when the natural flow of emotions is obstructed—with shaming admonitions to "quit being a crybaby" or "take it like a man," or by punishing children for showing emotions—the natural mending process becomes interrupted and blocked. Access to authentic emotions is foundational to a healthy, vital life, and I consider it the most important pursuit an adult can undertake. It is for this reason that one of the main themes of this book is my work to reclaim my ability to feel.

A final topic for this section is forgiveness. In popular culture, forgiveness is often presented in this way:

Forgiving = Good

Not Forgiving = Bad

Like many other people, I used to hold this black-and-white view, and it kept me stuck in a no-win dynamic. When I tried to forgive, it often felt like a lie or a simplistic fix for a complex issue. If I didn't forgive, it nagged at me and felt toxic.

My perspective underwent a profound shift after I discovered the work of Dr. Janis Abrahms Spring, a clinical psychologist and nationally recognized expert on issues of trust, intimacy, and forgiveness. In *How Can I Forgive You? The Courage to Forgive, The Freedom Not To*, she delineates four categories of forgiveness—two healthy and two unhealthy—instead of two.

The Four Approaches to Forgiveness
(Reprinted with permission from Dr. Janis Abrahms Spring)

- **Cheap forgiveness** (unhealthy) is a quick and easy pardon with no processing of emotion and no coming to terms with the injury. It is premature, superficial, and undeserved. It is an unconditional, unilateral, often compulsive attempt at peacekeeping.

- **Refusing to forgive** (unhealthy) is a reactive, rigid, often compulsive response to violation that cuts the hurt party off from life and leaves him or her stewing in his or her own hostile juices. It is a decision to continue to punish the offender and reject reconciliation, even if that decision also punishes the hurt party.

- **Acceptance** (healthy) is a responsible, authentic response to an interpersonal injury when the offender can't or won't engage in the healing process—when he or she is unwilling or unable to make good. It is a program of self-care, a generous and healing gift to oneself, accomplished by the self, for the self. It asks nothing of the offender.

- **Genuine forgiveness** (healthy) is a hard-won transaction, an intimate dance between two people bound together by an interpersonal violation. As the offender works hard to earn forgiveness through genuine, generous acts of repentance and restitution, the hurt party works hard to let go of his or her resentment and need for retribution. Together they redress the injury.

Although I didn't learn of Dr. Spring's work until more than a decade after my father died, my healing journey was informed by a desire to address the issue of forgiveness in a thorough rather than a knee-jerk way. I followed the trail of my inner process as attentively as I was able, groping in the dark for each next step. After reading *How Can I Forgive You?* I gained a greater understanding of how my intuitive process had been guiding me toward a full resolution with my father. I was grateful for Dr. Spring's clear, eloquent distinctions, which allowed me to reflect on my journey and deal with a number of loose ends. I learned that this work can be done years or even decades after the loss of a loved one. Revisiting old hurts that may have been patched up instead of fully addressed can lead to deeper levels of healing.

APPENDIX C

Recommended Resources

Grief, Loss, and Life Transitions

Brooks, Jane. *Midlife Orphan: Facing Life's Changes Now That Your Parents Are Gone.* New York: Berkley Books, 1999.

Chethik, Neil. *Fatherloss: How Sons of All Ages Come to Terms with the Deaths of Their Dads.* New York: Hyperion, 2001.

Chodron, Pema. *When Things Fall Apart: Heart Advice for Difficult Times.* Boston: Shambhala Publications, Inc., 2005.

Greenspan, Miriam. *Healing Through the Dark Emotions: The Wisdom of Grief, Fear, and Despair.* Boston: Shambhala Publications, Inc., 2004.

Kennedy, Alexandra. *The Infinite Thread: Healing Relationships Beyond Loss.* Hillsboro, OR: Beyond Words Publishing, Inc., 2001.

———. *Losing a Parent: Passage to a New Way of Living.* San Francisco: HarperSanFrancisco, 1991.

Lesser, Elizabeth. *Broken Open: How Difficult Times Can Help Us Grow.* New York: Villard, 2004.

Levy, Alexander. *The Orphaned Adult: Understanding and Coping with Grief and Change After the Death of Our Parents.* Reading, MA: Perseus Books, 1999.

McClelland, Carol L. *The Seasons of Change: Using Nature's Wisdom to Grow Through Life's Inevitable Ups and Downs.* Berkeley, CA: Conari Press, 1998.

Myers, Edward. *When Parents Die: A Guide for Adults.* New York: Penguin Books USA, Inc., 1997.

Schuurman, Donna. *Never the Same: Coming to Terms with the Death of a Parent.* New York: St. Martin's Press, 2003.

Secunda, Victoria. *Losing Your Parents, Finding Your Self.* New York: Hyperion, 2000.

Child Abuse Recovery

Gil, Eliana. *Outgrowing the Pain: A Book For and About Adults Abused as Children.* New York: Dell Publishing, 1983.

Mellody, Pia. *Facing Codependence.* San Francisco: Harper & Row, 1989.

Miller, Alice. *Breaking Down the Wall of Silence: The Liberating Experience of Facing Painful Truth.* New York: Meridian, 1993.

————. *The Drama of the Gifted Child: The Search for the True Self,* Revised Edition. New York: Basic Books, Inc., 1996.

————. *For Your Own Good: Hidden Cruelty in Child-Rearing and the Roots of Violence.* New York: Farrar, Straus and Giroux, 1983.

————. *Thou Shalt Not Be Aware: Society's Betrayal of the Child.* New York: Farrar, Straus and Giroux, 1981.

Napier, Nancy. *Getting Through the Day: Strategies for Adults Hurt as Children.* New York: W. W. Norton & Company, 1993.

————. *Recreating Your Self.* New York: W. W. Norton & Company, 1990.

Scarf, Maggie. *Secrets, Lies, Betrayals: How the Body Holds the Secrets of a Life, and How to Unlock Them.* New York: Random House, 2004.

Whitfield, Charles L. *Healing the Child Within: Discovery and Recovery for Adult Children of Dysfunctional Families.* Deerfield Beach, FL: Health Communications, Inc., 1989.

Forgiveness

Safer, Jeanne. *Forgiving & Not Forgiving: A New Approach to Resolving Intimate Betrayal.* New York: Avon Books, 1999.

Spring, Janis Abrahms. *How Can I Forgive You? The Courage to Forgive, the Freedom Not To.* New York: HarperCollins Publishers Inc., 2005.

Weisel, Elie, Thich Nhat Hanh, Thomas Moore, and Marianne Williamson. *The Power of Forgiveness,* DVD. Directed by Martin Doblmeier. New York: First Run Features, 2007.

Active Imagination

Hannah, Barbara. *Encounters with the Soul: Active Imagination as Developed by C.G. Jung.* Santa Monica, CA: Sigo Press, 1981.

Johnson, Robert. *Inner Work: Using Dreams & Active Imagination for Personal Growth.* San Francisco: Harper & Row, 1986.

Subpersonalities

Internal Family Systems Therapy:

Schwartz, Richard C. *Introduction to the Internal Family Systems Model.* Oak Park, IL: Trailheads Publications, 2001.

————. *You Are the One You've Been Waiting For: Bringing Courageous Love to Intimate Relationships.* Oak Park, IL: Trailheads Publications, 2008.

The Center for Self Leadership (the official IFS organization) http://www.selfleadership.org
In-person and telephone practitioners, workshops, trainings, conferences, books, and other resources

Other subpersonalities resources:

Brown, Molly Young. *Growing Whole: Self-Realization on an Endangered Planet.* Mt. Shasta, CA: Psychosynthesis Press, 2009.

Ferrucci, Piero. *What We May Be: Techniques for Psychological and Spiritual Growth Through Psychosynthesis.* New York: Jeremy P. Tarcher, 1982.

Firman, John, & Ann Gila. *Psychosynthesis: A Psychology of the Spirit.* Albany, NY: State University of New York Press, 2002.

Stone, Hal, & Sidra Stone. *Embracing Our Selves: The Voice Dialogue Manual.* San Rafael, CA: New World Library, 1998.

Art Therapy and Process Art

Capacchione, Lucia. *The Art of Emotional Healing.* Boston: Shambhala Publications, Inc., 2001.

———. *The Creative Journal: The Art of Finding Yourself.* North Hollywood, CA: Newcastle Publishing Co., Inc., 1989.

———. *Recovery of Your Inner Child: The Highly Acclaimed Method for Liberating Your Inner Self.* New York: Simon & Schuster, 1991.

Cassou, Michele, & Stewart Cubley. *Life, Paint and Passion: Reclaiming the Magic of Spontaneous Expression.* New York: Jeremy P. Tarcher, 1995.

Diaz, Adriana. *Freeing the Creative Spirit: Drawing on the Power of Art to Tap the Magic and Wisdom Within.* San Francisco: Harper SanFrancisco, 1992.

Ganim, Barbara, & Susan Fox. *Visual Journaling: Going Deeper Than Words.* Wheaton, IL: Quest Books, 1999.

Malchiodi, Cathy A. *The Art Therapy Sourcebook.* Los Angeles: Lowell House, 1998.

———. *The Soul's Palette: Drawing on Art's Transformative Powers for Health and Well-Being.* Boston: Shambhala Publications, Inc., 2002.

Williams, Heather. *Drawing as a Sacred Activity: Simple Steps to Explore Your Feelings and Heal Your Consciousness.* Novato, CA: New World Library, 2002.

The Painting Experience
http://www.processarts.com
Process art workshops, retreats, study groups, and individual mentoring

Journaling

Berg, Elizabeth. *Escaping into the Open: The Art of Writing True.* New York: HarperCollins Publishers, Inc., 1999.

DeSalvo, Louise. *Writing as a Way of Healing: How Telling Our Stories Transforms Our Lives.* San Francisco: HarperSanFrancisco, 1999.

Jacobs, Beth. *Writing for Emotional Balance: A Guided Journal to Help You Manage Overwhelming Emotions.* Oakland, CA: New Harbinger Publications, 2005.

Johnson, Alexandra. *Leaving a Trace: On Keeping a Journal: The Art of Transforming a Life into Stories.* Boston: Little, Brown and Company, 2001.

Communication

Campbell, Susan. *Getting Real: Ten Truth Skills You Need to Live an Authentic Life.* Tiburon, CA: H. J. Kramer/New World Library, 2001.

―――――. *Saying What's Real: 7 Keys to Authentic Communication and Relationship Success.* Tiburon, CA: H. J. Kramer/New World Library, 2005.

Rosenberg, Marshall B. *Nonviolent Communication: A Language of Life.* 2nd ed. Encinitas, CA: Puddledancer Press, 2003.

High Sensitivity

Aron, Elaine N. *The Highly Sensitive Person: How to Thrive When the World Overwhelms You.* New York: Broadway Books, 1996.

———. *The Highly Sensitive Child: Helping Our Children Thrive When the World Overwhelms Them.* New York: Broadway Books, 2002.

———. *The Highly Sensitive Person in Love: Understanding and Managing Relationships When the World Overwhelms You.* New York: Broadway Books, 2000.

———. *The Highly Sensitive Person's Workbook.* New York: Broadway Books, 1999.

Zeff, Ted. *The Highly Sensitive Person's Survival Guide: Essential Skills for Living Well in an Overstimulating World.* Oakland, CA: New Harbinger Publications, Inc., 2004.

Other

The Findhorn Foundation
http://www.findhorn.org
Spiritual community, learning center, and ecovillage

Hancock, Emily. *The Girl Within: A Groundbreaking New Approach to Female Identity.* New York: Fawcett Columbine, 1989.

Zukav, Gary. *The Seat of the Soul.* New York: Simon & Schuster, 1989.

Acknowledgments

Enormous thanks are extended to my sister Kathie for her generosity and skill in streamlining my writing through countless incarnations and for her unswerving faith in my work.

Gratitude is also extended to my mother, whose commitment to my father prompted me to dig more deeply within myself to clarify issues and portray him accurately and respectfully. I learned the importance of including background material to describe the culture and values out of which he came, particularly regarding the treatment of children. I'm also grateful to her for being willing to read several drafts of this book, answer countless questions, and repeatedly revisit the pain of her loss and the turbulence of our family life to assist me as I wrote.

I am also grateful to the following people:

My father's sister, Rose Wayne, for hours of oral history interviews, for helping bring to life pieces of family history, for frequently quoting her mother's words "Every pot has a lid" and always holding out hope that I'd find my life partner, and for our precious connection;

Roger Easterbrooks, for launching my quest for embodiment;

Brant Cortright, for insightful supervision and support during graduate school and for recommending Paul Bowman as a therapist;

Phil Tomlinson, who shared with me about losing his father and inspired me to experience my loss as deeply as possible;

Judy Vida, who drew on my experience during the illness and death of her daughter, Jo Hana Goldberg, and strengthened my belief that this book might be of use to readers;

Janis Berwitt, Terry Sims, and Liz Coblentz, for supporting me well around the time of my father's death;

Dick Schwartz, for developing the Internal Family Systems Model, which has been instrumental in my healing since 2007, and to IFS trainers Toni Herbine-Blank, Chris Mathna, Kay Gardner, Susan McConnell, and Paul Ginter for support and insights;

Ellen Kleiner, Priscilla Long, and Margaret Diehl, for outstanding editorial critiques;

And Vern Haddick, WH, Janis Berwitt, Don Martin, Bill Dinardo, Sheila Ciccaglione, and Jenny Lloyd, for editorial feedback and encouragement.

Profound thanks are also extended to my father's primary medical team at Mt. Sinai Medical Center in Cleveland, Ohio—Drs. Vladimir Vekstein, Gerald Grossman, Mark Botham, and Louis Priem—who brought great heart to their work and whose respect, commitment, and professionalism helped create a caring environment for my father's last days.

Finally, love and gratitude as big as the Milky Way to my husband, Charlie Alolkoy, for creative assistance, for patience and perceptive feedback while I wrote, for sharing my vision of equality and mutual respect, for walking his talk and being a model of love in action, for uplifting me and inspiring me to be my best self, and for being a far more wonderful life partner than my wildest dreams could have possibly imagined.

About the Author

Kira Freed, MA, LPC, BCC, is a licensed mental health counselor, certified life and wellness coach, and freelance writer who holds two master's degrees, one in integral counseling psychology from the California Institute of Integral Studies and the other in anthropology from the University of Colorado–Boulder. She also holds a certificate in nonfiction writing from the University of Washington–Seattle and has completed Levels 1–3 professional trainings in the Internal Family Systems Model.

In addition to doing therapy with individuals and couples, Kira has cofacilitated women's self-discovery groups that combine expressive arts, journaling, and guided imagery. Her current human development work is a blend of life and wellness coaching with the Internal Family Systems Model.

Kira has written more than 175 books for educational publishers, including Learning A–Z, Benchmark Education, Wright Group/McGraw-Hill, Rosen Publishing, and Zaner-Bloser. The books, written at graduated levels of complexity, are used to teach elementary schoolchildren to read while introducing them to high-interest content. Topics range from nonfiction subjects such as history, biography, and life science to a fictionalized third-grade adaptation of *Losing and Finding My Father* titled *Losing Grandpa*.

Kira lives in Tucson, Arizona, with her husband, Charlie Alolkoy, an artist. She can be reached at:

http://www.losingandfindingmyfather.com
http://www.kirafreedcoaching.com